CHRISTOPH PUETZ

Net Services USA LLC

The Web Hosting Manager

The Web Hosting Manager

© Christoph Puetz
3780 West Bucknell Drive
Highlands Ranch, CO, 80129
Phone 303.525.5059
www.netservicesusa.com

About the Author

Christoph Puetz is an international author and owner of a successful small business.

At the time of this writing, Christoph has successfully published books east and west of the Atlantic Ocean and sold several thousand copies of his books. More publications are in development as you read.

Christoph currently lives in Colorado where his business is located.

Foreword

Running a Web Hosting Business.

In early 2002, I started my own Web hosting business. I thought I knew it all and nothing could stop me. Boy, was I wrong. Now more than three years later, I am much more knowledgeable and have much more experience under my belt. Am I still a Web host? Yes, I am. I am providing Web hosting to a hand-selected group of clients. However, Web hosting is no longer my core business. By going through the process of building a Web hosting business from the ground up I learned a lot about myself. This knowledge helped me to re-design my business model and to become more successful.

This book will provide you with a great amount of information for starting and operating a Web hosting business. But that is not all. I will also give you a look behind the scenes of my own business, talk about business strategy and how to aim for success. I was almost to the point of shutting down my business but then I re-energized and was able to motivate myself to get going again.

By the time this book hits the market my business will have celebrated its third anniversary and is heading towards a promising future. I enjoy operating my business and things are looking great. Even though I work very long hours every day I enjoy the opportunities my own business is able to provide.

I hope I am able to share a little bit of this with this book.

Best regards,

Christoph Puetz

Owner Net Services USA LLC

Table of Contents

What is Web Hosting?

W eb hosting is the business of providing the server storage, Internet connectivity, and services necessary to serve files and images for a Web site.

Web host: A company that provides Web hosting services is called a Web host, and their services of server storage, Internet connectivity, and services are called Web hosting plans. There are literally thousands (maybe even hundreds of thousands) of Web hosting companies which offer these services to the public. The size of these companies range anywhere from individuals to worldwide corporations.

Domain name: A domain name is the unique name that identifies an Internet Web site. Domain names always have two or more parts, separated by dots. The part on the left is the more specific (the actual name), and the part on the right is the more general.

Reseller: A Web hosting reseller purchases a hosting package from a regular or specialized Web host and resells the Web hosting service under his own brand name.

Data center: A data center is a highly secure, fault-resistant facility housing customer equipment that connects to telecommunications networks. These facilities accommodate Web servers, switches, routers, and racks. Data centers support corporate Web sites and as an example provide server locations for Web hosting companies.

Does This Light Your Fire?

Do Web servers give you the warm fuzzies? Does the thought of routers and racks make you feel more structured? Do you look at a Web host and think: "Heck, I can do this better!" Are you ready for a change in your life or at least a healthy challenge? Do you want to get away from the corporate rat race? Then maybe Web hosting is for you!

But how can you know beforehand without getting in too deep or letting lost down the wrong path?

That is what this book is for – it is your first step in doing the homework you need to start up a Web hosting business.

The next chapter will give you a list of 20 basic steps that can jump start you into the business. After that, the chapters go into various levels of detail in different topics where there are no limits to how far you can develop yourself. I finish the book up with my own story, so you can see it isn't always easy but it can be done!

So let's get to it!

Steps to build a Web Hosting Business

L et's build a Web hosting business from the ground up. I will show you what you need to do to get started. Every step will include the costs associated with it so that you can see for yourself how easy and affordable it can be to start this kind of Internet business.

You do not need millions of dollars, not even thousands of dollars to get going.

This chapter lists and then gives short but sweet advice for the main 20 steps that you need to get started.

Step by Step – Our Quick Start List

1). Come up with a company name. Make sure it is not trademarked or taken already.

2). Find a matching domain name for your business.

3). Register your business with your state and local authorities. Decide on the legal form.

4). Open a bank account. Deposit startup funds.

5). Decide which services and what hosting packages to offer.

6). Sign up for a domain name reseller account.

7). Find a reseller Web host or lease/rent/buy a server with a Web control panel included or as an add-on.

8). Design product packages.

9). Build/design a Web site.

10). Sign up for a credit card merchant account or third party credit card processing provider. Implement domain name reselling except billing and credit card processing (see step 11 before deciding).

11). Decide if you are building your own tools for the sign-up process or if you would rather purchase billing/account setup software. Purchase software as necessary.

12). Purchase a SSL certificate.

13). Implement SSL for the signup process on your Web site.

14). Design and order business cards.

15). List your Web site with search engines and hosting directories.

16). Setup a helpdesk (optional: and create a support section with tutorials and F.A.Q.).

17). Have friends or family members test your Web site for complete functionality. Fix problems.

18). Design a marketing campaign and decide on where to do your marketing. Schedule your marketing efforts. Check for deadlines with publishers.

19). Hire staff and/or make additional preparations for customer support (remote e-mail solutions, cell phone, etc.).

20). Setup an accounting solution; hire an accountant, or make other preparations for your bookkeeping.

Your business is up and running and soon the first clients will be signing up. Sounds easy, doesn't it. There is much more to it than what our quick start list can provide. This book will guide you through the steps necessary but it will not take away all the work. Each startup situation is different and you will have to invest a lot of work before the first customer signs up.

An Original Company Name

Not Trademarked or Taken Already

Every business needs a name to be identifiable. This means that you need to think about what name you should use as your business name. You can either select a descriptive name like "John Doe Web Hosting, Inc." or something more generic, like "JD, Inc.". Do thorough research for the state you are located in. Check Internet and public registers to make sure the name is not already taken.

You should also consider whether to restrict your business to only Web hosting or whether you would like to offer different services under the same business name. A business name that does not limit you to a certain industry can be the better option. Plan and choose carefully. It is much easier to make adjustments before you actually start your business.

Since I am located in Colorado, the best place for someone like me to start research would be the state government. The appropriate Web site for checking the public register can be found here:

   http://www.sos.state.co.us/biz/InquiryMenu.doc

Another non-official place for a name search is in the Yellow Pages. For Colorado, you should direct your browser to:

   http://www.dexonline.com

In whichever state you live, do your homework and find out what the options for your state of residency are when it comes to choosing a good name for your business.

Be sure to stay away from anything that could cause you legal trouble. Please do not go with a name like *Miicroosoft*. ;-) Be unique.

Costs associated with this step: $0.00

The Right Domain Name

Once you have found the right business name for your new venture, you need to check for a matching domain name. If the business name has a matching domain name available - perfect. Register the name as soon as possible. The longer you wait, the greater the chance that somebody else may have registered it in the mean time.

Where is a good place to register a domain name? There are several domain registration Web sites available on the Internet. But since we are trying to keep our costs low and at the same time still keeping an eye on quality, I recommend giving https://domains.ev1servers.net a try for the domain name registration (at least for this step).

Costs associated with this step: $6.49

Total Cost: $6.49 (including this step)

Register Your Business

By now, you have a good business name and a great domain name. And finally you are ready to take the first step in officially operating a business; it is time for you to register your business with the state and local authorities.

There are several legal forms of doing business to choose from:

- DBA – "Doing business as"

- LLC – "Limited Liability Company"

- Form a corporation

I recommend the "LLC" for the following reasons:

Limited Liability Company (LLC)

A Limited Liability Company is designed to provide the limited liability features of a corporation and the tax efficiencies and operational flexibility of a sole proprietorship and partnership. The actual formation is a little more complex and more formal than that of a sole proprietorship and/or partnership. A LLC does have members but can also be formed by just one person (one member). Basically, a LLC receives the corporation's protection from personal liability for business debts and the tax structure of partnerships and sole proprietorships.

The advantages of a Limited Liability Company (LLC):

- Members have limited liability.

- Actual taxation might be more beneficial for the members.

- Business form looks more professional than a sole proprietorship in many cases.

- A LLC only needs one member.

The disadvantages of a Limited Liability Company (LLC):

- A LLC cannot seek funding by offering shares to shareholders.

- The liability protection can be removed by a judge if it is obvious that the members did not run the business as a LLC but as a partnership / sole proprietorship.

- Less laws that govern the LLC. This could be a problem in complicated business situations.

Each state is set up differently and has different requirements. You need to check for your state.

For example, the fees for the state of Colorado can be found here:

http://www.sos.state.co.us/pubs/info_center/fees7_01_04.htm

In Colorado, you can register your business online here:

http://www.sos.state.co.us/pubs/business/update09_15_04.htm

Costs associated with this step: $50.00 (online)

Total Cost: $56.49 (including this step)

The Bank Account and Startup Funds

You are on your way. You have just founded your own business!

You now have everything you will need to go on to the next step: Opening a free business bank account. I opened my own business checking account with US Bank. They have offices in many convenient locations, offer Internet banking, give you a free Visa Check card, and, best of all, the bank account is free of charge (Basic version, which is more than sufficient for any startup).

Assuming that you registered a LLC, you can use your own social security number for the bank account and the business. This is absolutely legit and ok as long as you are the only member of the LLC.

http://www.usbank.com/cgi_w/cfm/small_business/products_and_services/checking/checking_acct_comp_sb.cfm

http://www.usbank.com

Check with your house bank or other local banks to see if they offer similar services at no charge. You can now take your own startup funds and deposit them into the checking account.

Costs associated with this step: $0.00

Money spent so far: $56.49

Which Services and What Hosting Packages

Now comes the more difficult part. You have to decide what services and products you want to offer. As you are starting a Web hosting business, "Web Hosting" should be one of your products, right?! But every Web site also needs a domain name. Do you want to resell domain names, too? Reselling domain names helps tie customers to your business. I highly recommend adding it as an optional service to your business.

How about Web design? Can you build and design Web sites? How about IT consulting services? Do you know computers? Can you service and troubleshoot them?

Don't worry too much about the Web hosting part and the domain names. I'll show you how that works. But if you have skills in any of the other areas. it could be well worth adding these products to your business and business plan. Or if you have friends or family who can design Web sites, you could "resell" their services or work out a referral program and make some money by referring customers to them. Think about this out for a while, then decide.

Costs associated with this step: $0.00

Money spent so far: $56.49 (including this step)

The Domain Name Reseller Account

Reselling domain names is a very resource-friendly business and can be very lucrative over time. It is not something you get rich with quick, but it adds a steady stream of income to your business. Most of the time, clients stay with the company they register their domain with for the life time of the domain name.

Now you are a Web host. Is domain reselling the right thing for you? In most cases, it is. It adds value to your business. You can provide a one-stop solution to your customers. The customer buys the domain name he wants and then needs hosting. If you offer both at reasonable prices and with no fuss, you might just have won a new customer.

If the customer has to go somewhere else to buy a domain name, he might come across different Web hosting offers along the way. Can you risk losing this customer with no chance of getting him back? If you need the business and want to increase your customer base, you cannot risk letting this customer go elsewhere. If you have a different business model, you might think otherwise. But for most Web hosts, the following remains the norm: once the customer leaves to buy a domain name somewhere else, he will not be coming back.

Reselling domain names is easy. In many cases, the registrar provides you with the tools you need. In other cases, you have to purchase a third party product to get going.

Often you can code your own solution and tie it into the registry's API. As mentioned before, if your solution is automated properly, you won't have much work to do.

The **Free** Enom Domain Reseller Account

We recommend Enom, Inc. for domain name reselling. It is easy to use and you get very low prices right from the start. We can set you up with a free Enom, Inc. domain name reseller account. You can start reselling domain names based on the low **$8.95** wholesale price that you get from Enom.

There are no costs associated with obtaining this reseller account and it only takes a few minutes to sign up. Signup instructions can be found on our Web site

http://www.webhostingreport.net/domains/form.php

Costs associated with this step: $0.00

Money spent so far: $56.49 (including this step)

The Reseller Web Hosting Account

Finally, we're getting to the good stuff. It is time to sign you up for a reseller Web hosting account. What is a reseller hosting account at all?

For you as the newcomer, a reseller account is your way to break into this industry without having to know any system administration or how to fix a Web server. A reseller hosting account lets you create your own hosting accounts under your main account, meaning you can take on customers and set them up with their own Web hosting account at their domain. You will have a certain amount of bandwidth and disk space available and can split it into small pieces and resell them at a profit. Compare it to a wholesale/retail business. You buy Web hosting wholesale and sell it to clients retail.

Advantages

The major advantage of reseller hosting accounts is that you need almost no technical knowledge to start out with. The actual Web host you buy your reseller account from will take care of all the technical issues and the system administration for you. You receive support requests from your clients and pass them on to your Web host as needed. He takes care of the issue and lets you know when things are back on track. You then go back to the client and tell him that the issue has been taken care of. The client does not even know that there is another company in the background. You will be able to fix some things from your master Web control panel yourself.

The second major advantage of this business model is that you will learn quite a bit from your reseller Web host. Every support ticket or issue is also a learning experience for you. You will gain superior technical knowledge in no time. Of course, it always helps if you already have some Web hosting-related experience. But if you're just starting out, it is always nice to have someone covering your back and taking care things you are not familiar with.

I recommend a reseller host who also has a customer forum for support and for building a community. You can chat with others in the same situation and learn from them, too. It has never been that easy to build a business in a new industry by following a path like this. But your risk is minimal. All you basically need to take care of is customer service and billing. What more could you want?

Recommendations

The following businesses have been evaluated AND used by me at some point in the past. They might not be the cheapest option out there (but neither are they expensive), but as a newbie, you will want world-class backend support and these companies provide it.

http://www.httpme.com

http://www.voxtreme.com

http://www.site5.com

This step will cost you a monthly fee that you will need to take into account from now on. Use your credit card to signup and dedicate yourself to this venture (you can always back out. No year-long contract or obligation is required). From this moment on, you have to be certain that you really want to take a shot at this because you will be spending money. But the associated risk is small, and the monthly fees are acceptable, and if you work for your business, it will be easy to make up for the money.

Costs associated with this step (approximately):
   $35.00 per month

Money spent so far: $56.49 (one-time)

Money spent so far: $35.00 (monthly)

Design Your Product Packages

Now we need to figure out what hosting packages you can sell from our reseller Web hosting package. This is rather important as it will be the part where you plant the seeds of how much money you will make.

Your Target Customers

One important thing upfront: as a newcomer to the hosting business, you will have to work with lower prices in the beginning if your target customers on the Internet. If you are going after the local market, you can work with normal (or higher prices) right away. Local customers tend to compare less and would rather pay a little more and deal with the local 'guy'. Your options depend on where you live. If you live in a rural area with few businesses and potential clients around, you will need to look on the Internet for clients. If you live in a medium to large metropolitan area, you can try the local route.

Overselling

It's a known industry fact that most customers will never use all their resources. It is safe to assume that the clients will maybe use 75% of the resources purchased. For you as the Web host, this means that you can sell more resources than what you actually have. Be sure that your Web host allows you to upgrade your own package if you reach the limit.

Packages

It is always good to offer at least 3 different packages for the client to choose from. Variety helps attract clients.

Internet Prices (The Liberal Approach) and the Numbers Game

Let's assume you are buying a reseller package with 2 GB disk space and 20 GB traffic allowance (bandwidth). By practicing the principle of overselling, you could sell the following packages and barely run the risk of reaching your limits at all.

Package "A" with 50 MB disk space + 3 GB bandwidth - $3.99

Package "B" with 100 MB disk space + 5 GB bandwidth - $6.99

Package "C" with 250 MB disk space + 8 GB bandwidth - $8.99

Package "B" with 100 MB disk space + 5 GB bandwidth - $6.99

Package "C" with 250 MB disk space + 8 GB bandwidth - $8.99

Example A: Let's assume you sell 20 Packages "A". This would give you an income before cost ($35.00) of $79.80 or a net profit of $44.80. Not bad, isn't it!? Now let's add 20% overselling to this approach. That means you make an additional $15.96 on top of the $79.80 (= $95.76).

Example B: Let's assume you sell 10 Packages "A" and 10 Packages "B". This would give you an income before costs ($35.00) of $109.80 or a net profit of $74.80. Not bad, isn't it!? Now let's add only 10% overselling to this approach. That means you generate an additional $10.98 on top of the $109.80 (= $120.78).

So, you can play the numbers game and also keep an eye on the resource usage of your clients. In most cases, you will be able to add additional 20% on top of the estimates here. I have been able to generate income of almost $250.00 on a single reseller account ($35.00) and my clients used only a fraction of their resources.

Important: Once you have acquired about 30-40 clients, you should raise your prices for all new customers. You are here to make money, right?! Raise the prices slowly and clients should still sign up. A dollar per quarter is a reasonable approach.

Local Prices

Let's assume you buy a reseller package with 2 GB disk space and 20 GB traffic allowance (bandwidth). By practicing the principle of overselling, you could sell the following packages and barely run the risk of reaching your limits at all..

Package "A" with 25 MB disk space + 2 GB bandwidth - $9.99

Package "B" with 100 MB disk space + 5 GB bandwidth - $16.99

Package "C" with 250 MB disk space + 8 GB bandwidth - $21.99

Package "B" with 100 MB disk space + 5 GB bandwidth - $16.99

Package "C" with 250 MB disk space + 8 GB bandwidth - $21.99

Example A: Let's assume you sell 20 Packages "A". This would give you an income before costs ($35.00) of $199.80 or a net profit of $164.80. Not bad, isn't it!? Now let's add 20% overselling to this approach. That means you generate an additional $39.96 on top of the $199.80 (= $239.76).

Now look at this margin.. The best thing is that other local providers charge even twice as much as the prices listed here and still find clients.

The only problem with the higher prices is that it takes a little longer to get the clients. But in the long run the higher prices will carry you much further. A good strategy is to find clients with low prices first and then change the strategy. Or you can operate two Web sites: one for Internet clients with lower prices and a marketing strategy for the Internet, and a second site with higher prices and a local marketing strategy.

Costs associated with this step (max): $0.00 per month

Money spent so far: $56.49 (one-time)

Money spent so far: $35.00 (monthly)

Design and Build a Web Site

Now that you have worked on your hosting packages and also have a reseller Web hosting account, it is time to build a Web site. You should have something like FrontPage., FrontPage Express, Adobe GoLive or Macromedia Dreamweaver to build and modify your Web sites. These, of course, aren't your only options but they are well know and there is a lot of material for them on the Web to help you. If you don't have these tools, ask friends or family. In most cases, you can get the software for free from them anyway. Make sure you verify the license agreement if necessary.

Templates

The easiest way to create a Web site is by using templates. Check out the following site.

> http://www.aplustemplates.com

This company offers a low-cost way to get access to some of the finest Web site templates on the Internet. And the best thing is, access to all these templates is very affordable. For $29.95 per year, you gain access to 150+ Web site templates. Most of the templates are easy to modify. All you need is some text.

If you do not want to build your own Web site, you can ask somebody else to do it. Post your request here:

> http://www.sitepoint.com/forums/forumdisplay.php?f=7

Somebody will definitely do it for you. You will need to spend some money, though.

You can also check out our own little template store. It's nothing special, but you can purchase high quality Web site templates at very affordable prices.

> http://www.purchaseatemplate.com

Web Site Content

What do you need to fill the pages with text? Look at other Web hosting sites for ideas. You do not need much to start and getting ideas from other Web sites might be the best start. One of our reseller host recommendations (httpme.com) even allows you to use the information from their Web site. Most reseller hosts will also let you use their ToS (terms of service) and their data center info. That's almost everything you need to get started. You can add tutorials, FAQs, and other things later. Make sure you build a nice support section for your Web site. If your reseller host offers the "Fantastico" script for the "cpanel" control panel, you can install a fully automated helpdesk system as an example - for free (it comes with the package).

Don't be shocked when you see the high-tech Web sites of some of the other Web hosts. Many of these sites look just like the others and nothing stands out. Sometimes the simple approach is the better one. The client will easily find all the information he needs. And you can always work on your site when you have a little time. The important thing is a clean and easy to navigate Web site to start with.

Costs associated with this step: $29.95 (one-time)

Money spent so far: $86.44 (one-time)

Money spent so far: $35.00 (monthly)

The Credit Card Processor

Money, money, money ..... How are you going to collect it from your clients at all? Doing business locally allows you to accept payments via check. If you do business nationally or internationally (Internet), checks are not a good method of collecting payments from your clients.

So what do you do? You sign up for a credit card merchant account or third-party credit card processing provider.

A Real Credit Card Merchant

A full-blown credit card merchant account is much too expensive in the beginning, and the cost is simply not justified. But you can use third-party providers for credit card payments. You pay slightly higher transaction rates but this is a good way to start out.

Cheaper Options

I recommend signing up with PayPal or with 2Checkout. PayPal is free. 2Checkout.com has a low $49.00 sign-up fee. Both providers offer a complete suite of credit card tools for online merchants. Use one of these and you will be up and running soon.

You can then enter your products and each provider will provide the needed HTML code to implement into your Web site. It's very easy to do.

If implementing payment options into your Web site is too much of a hassle and you would rather automate the process, take a look at the section about credit card processing.

Costs associated with this step: $49.00 (one-time)

Money spent so far: $135.44 (one-time)

Money spent so far: $35.00 (monthly)

Credit Card Processing

Decide if you want to build your own tools for the sign-up process or if you would rather purchase billing or account setup software. Purchase software as necessary.

Instead of integrating the payment options directly onto your Web site, you can purchase ready-to-use software solutions for automating the whole process of signing up, credit card processing, and hosting account creation. Every step will be automated. You just have to approve each order and wait for the money to come in.

Finding Solutions

I recommend the following software packages. They will provide you with everything you need right out of the box. Yes, they cost a few dollars but the actual work time and the stress they will save you will probably be worth the money. You can also upgrade to this kind of solution later on. Just be aware that there are things out there that can help you immensely.

http://www.dramsystem.com
(Our favorite - we own a license, too)
$149.00 purchase or $14.95 leased

http://www.clientexec.com
$99.00 purchase or $9.95 leased

http://whoiscart.net
$35.00 purchase

Costs associated with this step (average): $99.00 (one-time)

Money spent so far: $234.44 (one-time)

Money spent so far: $35.00 (monthly)

Purchase an SSL Certificate

Do business on the Internet safely. You don't want to submit personal data over the Internet unless it is encrypted.

If you have gone with PayPal or 2Checkout for credit card payments, they provide the SSL encryption themselves. But if you use your own sign-up process for collecting customer data, you should implement a SSL certificate.

There are many different kinds available, but you do not need to spend money on the most expensive ones. A low-cost SSL certificate will do the job just fine.

Recommendations

I recommend the Starter SSL Certificate sold by EV1Servers:

http://www.ev1servers.net/english/starterssldetails.asp

At the time of this writing, they sell their certificates for a **$14.95 per year**. The normal price is around $20.00 per year. This is a fantastic deal. I purchased two of these certificates at $4.95 when they came out first, and I am very happy with the process and the price.

When calculating costs, I still use the regular price. I'd rather cover the worst-case scenario for you so that you know how much it can cost you to start your own Web hosting business, without hidden surprises.

Also see the next step for additional information.

Costs associated with this step (regular price): $20.00 (one-time)

Money spent so far: $254.44 (one-time)

Money spent so far: $35.00 (monthly)

Implement SSL in the Signup Process

Now it is time to put the new certificate to work. I recommend purchasing the SSL certificate for a URL similar to https://secure.yourdomain.com. This way, it will be very clear to your clients that you are a responsible Web host implementing a high level of security.

Your reseller Web host will help you get the SSL certificate installed and setup on the server. Pay close attention to how this is done since this might be a recurring situation if you have clients who need a certificate, too. In most cases, your Web host will do the setup for free.

Do not try to save money in the wrong places. Security and encryption on the Internet are important. Use your own SSL certificate to advertise your services and what you do to protect your customers from fraud. They will surely appreciate it.

Costs associated with this step: $0.00

Money spent so far: $254.44 (one-time)

Money spent so far: $35.00 (monthly)

Design and Order Business Cards

Most of your infrastructure has been setup and it is now time to think about the marketing stuff. I will start with the topic of business cards. Vista Print is one of the top providers when it comes to high quality, yet low-priced business cards.

Use the free or lowest-cost delivery option. I have never seen long delivery times. This will save you a lot of money. Make sure you select business cards that stand out from the crowd. Anything unusual will help your clients remember you. Use business cards whenever you can. This is a very affordable way to promote your business to potential customers.

Vista Print offers many specials. So read their Web site carefully to get the best deal on your new business cards from them.

Costs associated with this step: $19.99

Money spent so far: $274.43 (one-time)

Money spent so far: $35.00 (monthly)

Search Engine and Hosting Directory Listings

It is very important to get your Web site listed with some of the major search engines and Web hosting directories. You will need to do this when your actual Web site is ready for business and no longer looks like a big construction zone.

It will take a while for your site to appear on search engines, though. That's why you should get it listed as soon as possible.

Here is a list of directories for Web hosts:

http://www.hostinvestigator.com

http://www.4webhosting.com

http://www.webhostseek.com

http://www.hostindex.com

http://www.webhostlist.com

http://www.tophosts.com

http://www.ispcheck.com

http://www.hostingreviews.com

http://www.host-tribune.com

http://www.cyberwiser.com

http://www.hostfind.com

http://www.hostreview.com

http://www.findwebspace.com

http://www.hostspot.com

http://www.verihost.com

http://www.ihostcafe.com

http://www.hottesthost.com

http://www.webhostarea.com

http://www.hostcompare.com

http://www.reviewdepot.com

http://www.webhostdir.com

http://www.webhosters.com

http://www.hostfacts.com

Most search engines will find your Web site once you are listed in a few Web hosting directories. It is still a good idea to list your Web site with a few search engines yourself. Do not use a submission service though. You might get banned and not be listed.

Here is a short list of free search engines you can submit your site to:

http://www.dmoz.org (expect a one to two year delay before being listed)

http://www.altavista.com

http://www.alltheweb.com

http://www.altavista.com

http://www.alltheweb.com

Tip: First write a proper description for the directories and then copy and paste if from your master document. Do the same with the title and the URL. This will cut down submission time significantly.

Costs associated with this step: $0.00

Money spent so far: $274.43 (one-time)

Money spent so far: $35.00 (monthly)

Setup a Helpdesk / Support Section

Having Web hosting customers means that you also have to give them support options. Remember, as a reseller, you are able to pass on most of the support requests to your own reseller Web host and then return the results to your own customers. Of course, it is better if you can handle everything (or most of the requests) yourself. So always pay attention and be pro-active. Your rate of learning will be fast, and it will take only a short time to support your clients the way you want to, with world-class customer service. Remember, customer service is one of the keys to this business. You will not be successful if you fail here.

Helpdesks

I recommend a free helpdesk product to start out with. Unless you have bought one of the software packages mentioned in one of the earlier steps that includes a helpdesk, looking into a professional-looking helpdesk system is a good idea. I recommend the One or Zero Helpdesk (http://www.oneorzero.com).

The software is free and easy to install. The software maker also offers great support himself so that you can ask for assistance when working with the product.

You can also check out which scripts come with your own Web hosting account. Many of the newer control panel software packages offer the installation of free-to-use scripts, including helpdesk software. With the click of a few buttons, you could be up and running.

A Support Section (Optional)

Optional: Create a support section with tutorials and FAQs.

If you have enough time, you should start building up a knowledge base or FAQ (Frequently Asked Questions) section for your clients. This will help dramatically decrease the need for support. Instead of asking you, your customers will be able to help themselves up to a certain level by looking up the necessary information on your Web site.

What information will you need? It depends on which control panel you will be using as well as on what platform your reseller account will be hosted (example: Windows or Linux). Ask your own Web host what information on their Web site will they let you use and start off with that. Many reseller Web hosts specifically allow this in order to cut down on their own support costs.

Costs associated with this step: $0.00

Money spent so far: $274.43 (one-time)

Money spent so far: $35.00 (monthly)

Have Friends or Family Test Your Web Site

Your Web site is your business card on the Web. Make sure it is in perfect condition for your customers. No spelling errors should be visible and it should work in all different kinds of Web browsers (mainly Internet Explorer and Firefox). Ask friends and family to visit your Web site and look for broken links, spelling errors, and other things that might leave a bad taste with potential customers.

In most cases, friends and family are very supportive when somebody they know is starting their own business. Let them know that you can't pay for their work, but you will be able to offer them free or low-priced services down the road. They know that you are starting out and need all the support you can get.

You don't have any friends or family that can help? Ask around. Co-workers, neighbors, or even some folks on the Internet might help you out (look for forums that allow Web sites to be reviewed, usually in a special section of the forum). Perhaps offer some freebies or promise to pay them as soon as you make some money. Offer gift certificates.

Make sure you make a comprehensive list of all problem spots and fix them right away.

Costs associated with this step: $0.00

Money spent so far: $274.43 (one-time)

Money spent so far: $35.00 (monthly)

Design a Marketing Campaign

Design a marketing campaign and decide where to do marketing. Schedule your marketing efforts. Check for deadlines with publishers.

Marketing and advertising. You have to let the world know that you and your business are out there. If nobody knows, how will you get any customers at all?

There are several different ways to get customers. I will show you the basics so that you can find customers (also check out my marketing and advertising tips in a later section of this book). There is no easy way of advertising. It is a long process and the impact is usually pretty short-termed. If you stop advertising you will feel an immediate impact on the results. You will have fewer customer signups.

Word of Mouth
Ask friends and family to spread the word that you're open for business. Let them recommend your services to their friends, co-workers, and families. This is the most affordable way of advertising and one of the best. Once you have customers, ask them to recommend your services to their friends and family. If your clients are satisfied, they will be happy to recommend your business. Word of mouth is important. Perhaps offer referral fees to improve results.

Costs associated with this step: $0.00

Logowear
Go to http://www.cafepress.com and order a frame for your license plates, logo wear with your business slogan and logo. Wear this stuff when you go shopping or to the gym. This is a very affordable and long lasting way to advertise repeatedly. Approximate cost depends on what you order. For now, I will assume that you will spend about $75.00 on your own-branded merchandise.

Forums and Newsgroups

Become a member of one or more forums and newsgroups on the Internet. Use your forum signature to advertise your business services. Be sure to read up on the rules for each forum before doing this. Some do not allow this type of advertising, others promote it. Become an active poster and people will start asking for your advice and help, and may eventually become customers. This can become a very effective way of advertising.

Costs associated with this step: $0.00

Press Releases

Make use of free media reports. Publish a press release whenever possible. The occasion has to be noteworthy of course. Newspapers, magazines, radio and TV, they all receive press releases from the newswires. A local newspaper might catch on and will contact you to write a story about you and your business. Check out the business section of your local newspaper. How often do you see a report about a local business? Where I live, it happens quite often. Maybe the newspaper publishes company profiles every once in a while. Maybe you'll the chosen one.

How do you publish a press release? Find out how you can directly submit a press release to your local newspaper. It might require some work, but newspapers are always looking for information that they can publish. Use services like PRWeb.com to publish your press release. PRWeb.com even offers templates showing you what a professional press release looks like. You can even publish a press release free of cost with them.

Newspaper Advertising

Spend some money on local newspaper advertising. Ask for special rates for new businesses. Where I live, I can publish a business card-sized ad for about $90.00 in a weekly newspaper distributed to about 70,000 people. You should be able to find similar deals in your area, maybe even for less money. Run an ad for two weeks.

Costs associated with this step: $180.00

Local Business Directories

Go online and find business directories for your area and get listed. In most cases, this is free of charge. If the owner of a Web site wants a return link, setup a partner page on your Web site and link back. Both of you can then refer customers to each other.

Costs associated with this step: $0.00

Yellow Pages

Get listed in the local Yellow Pages. If there is one place for targeted advertising, it is in the Yellow Pages. Call the local phone company and find out what it will cost. My local phone company offered a small listing for just $10.00 a month.

Costs associated with this step: $10.00 (monthly)

Got print?

Got a printer at home? Make it work for you. Create flyers and distribute them. If local laws allow it, place them on telephone poles, bus stops, and other visible places. Otherwise, always place them (when parking your car somewhere) under the windshield wipers of the cars to the left and right of your car.

Costs associated with this step: $25.00

Online Advertising

Go online and search through newsgroups and forums for affordable advertising opportunities. Do not spend a fortune on one site. Rather spend the available money on three or four sites. Make sure that the sites you spend advertising money on are actually having traffic. The owner needs to show you traffic stats.

Costs associated with this step: $200.00

Visit Local Businesses

Create a small flyer or sales kit and visit local businesses. Talk to the owners and managers. Introduce yourself and leave the flyer with them. Call back the next day. You can also use the business cards you ordered earlier for this kind of advertising.

Costs associated with this step: $20.00

I just showed you 10 different ways of advertising. Some cost money and some don't. Make sure you always use several options at the same time to get the most out of your advertising. If your budget does not allow the expensive types of advertising, substitute them with the low-cost methods but in twice the amount. There is no one way to get to your potential customers. Be creative.

Costs associated with this step (one time / maximum): $500.00

Costs associated with this step (monthly): $10.00

Money spent so far: $774.43 (one-time)

Money spent so far: $45.00 (monthly)

Other Things to Take Care Of

Hire staff and/or make additional preparations for customer support (remote e-mail solutions, cell phone, etc.)

Well, you're in business now. The very first customer will sign up soon. You have already set up a support helpdesk, but are you monitoring the signup notifications and helpdesk tickets all the time? Make preparations so that you will be able to monitor everything. Sales requests, signups, support tickets, you need to be able to answer them in an acceptable time frame. If you are still employed somewhere else and have Internet access, perfect. But if not, you need to hire help or ask friends and family to help you out.

Effective Response System

Put a system in place that allows you to respond in an effective manner. An e-mail-enabled cell phone is a perfect choice if available. I personally would not sign up for it in the beginning unless I already had it. Stay away from adding unneeded costs to your business.

What can you do to get your business going and still work for your existing employer? Try to automate things. Automation makes it look like you are actually out there doing something, like running your business. If you are selling domain names, automate it. There are plenty of scripts and software packages out there that will do this for you. Setup helpdesk software that includes a knowledge base (see our advice earlier about this). Fill the knowledge base with knowledge and how-to information. Reduce the exposure of getting a helpdesk ticket for a simple question that isn't answered in your knowledge base.

If you cannot access your e-mail from work but you have access to your corporate e-mail, use forwarders on your own e-mail and have messages forwarded to work. At least you know what is going on and don't have to worry about open tickets or a new user signing-up. If worse comes to worst, you would be able to reply from the corporate address (though, I still do not recommend doing this if you can avoid it.) Ask friends for help. If you know somebody who has Web access during the day while you are at work and is willing to help out, forward the message to him or her. Prepare those friends with e-mail templates and instructions of what to do. A new account can be set up easily, maybe even via a script that your friend can execute with the information provided. You have to plan for these contingencies. Have some people you can trust lined up in case you need them. You could also check e-mail messages before you go to work. Visit a library at lunch for Internet access and check e-mail and work on tickets. As soon as you get home after work, dedicate some time to checking e-mail and working on tickets.

Costs associated with this step: $0.00

Money spent so far: $774.43 (one-time)

Money spent so far: $45.00 (monthly)

Accounting

Setup an accounting solution; hire an accountant, or make other preparations for your bookkeeping

You have already spent some money and, most likely, you will earn some money soon. Time to think about bookkeeping. If you know your way around a little bit and do not mind doing the number crunching yourself, a simple Excel spreadsheet can work well for a while. It is always hard to spend money when aren't making any. Anything free is good. Assuming that you have MS Office or the open-source solution Open Office, you are well on your way. This solution can be insufficient if you start experiencing fast growth, but it will carry you through the first year.

Software Packages

If you want to spend some money, consider Quicken or MS Money. They are affordable and will do the job just fine. For $79.00, you will get a good workable solution that is ready to grow with you.

If you want to spend more money, get QuickBooks or Peachtree accounting software. Or hire an accountant right away. I will leave that up to you. For the purpose of getting your business started with limited funds, I will use an Excel spreadsheet for our cost analysis.

Costs associated with this step: $0.00

Money spent so far: $774.43 (one-time)

Money spent so far: $45.00 (monthly)

Funding and Financing

E ven if a Web hosting business can, in some cases, be started on a shoestring, proper financing gives you a better start and better chances to make it through the first two years. As you probably know, most startup businesses fail within the first two years of their existence. You do not want to be one of them.

There are several ways for you to get financing or funds to start your business. The most common ones are:

- Money from savings and the income from your existing job

- Bank loan

- Venture capital

Personal Funds

Often an entrepreneur uses existing funds to start a business. Money taken from savings accounts or from other personal financial sources, are the best way to start your business. The only person you owe money to would be to yourself. Nobody can require you to do this and in a way different to how you want to do it. If you still have a job while starting your business, finance your business with the income from your job until you are ready to make the final step.

Bank Loans

Startup businesses without a credit history will have a hard time getting a credit card or a loan from a bank. If you as a person have good credit, you might be able to get the loan as an individual. Keep in mind that in this case, your personal assets are basically securing the loan. Depending on the amount of money, this can be risky. And as you know, banks won't hesitate to close the loan and hand it to a collection service if they feel their loan is at risk because you are not making your payments. This is not a good feeling. A bank loan also puts higher pressure on you to succeed. While some people have no problem handling this additional pressure, others do. If you know that you are one of these individuals, do not take out a bank loan to start your Web hosting venture.

Venture Capital

Unless you have really big plans, you will qualify to receive venture capital from any of the many venture capital providers out there. Don't even waste your time trying. These people do not fund small businesses where the ROI would be minimal for them. But there is venture capital out there that is available to you. It often even costs less than what you would have to pay elsewhere. Family members, friends, coworkers and business partners are all potential sources of venture capital to help you start or expand your existing small Web hosting business. The key is approaching them the right way.

The Important Questions

Draft the terms of your loan and review your payment schedule.

How much money do you need to borrow? What kind of fair interest rate would you be able to offer? Instead of paying interest, can you offer a share (for example, 5%) of the business? Or maybe you do want to ask for a loan. Can you offer an opportunity for investment?

When will you start repaying the loan, and over what period?

Identify potential lenders and investors.

Making the Proposal

Think about all the people you know who might be in a position to lend you money or who might be interested in investing into your business. It could be a relative, friend, and associate, just about anyone you know and trust. Prepare your proposal the same way you would if presenting your proposal to a bank or a real investor. You are asking for money. So make sure your request looks legit and professional.

Offer a fair deal and the necessary respect. Remember, the moment you ask, you need to convince your family (just as an example) that you are not that 22-year-old college dropout, but a business person who knows exactly what he or she wants.

You can e-mail your loan proposal to them along with a personal message. But that should only be done if they live far away and you cannot drive over to the person you are asking. Also do not surprise them out of the blue. Call ahead and make an "appointment" for when you would like to discuss something important with them and that you will e-mail them some information beforehand. Be professional.

If the person from whom you are going to request a loan or an investment lives within driving distance, drive out there. Set aside enough time and do not start asking the moment the door opens. Be polite, be professional. Explain your idea, present your business plan, and explain why you are there. Explain every step and thoroughly describe what you will do to pay back the investment or loan. Be prepared and also explain what you will do in case of failure. How will you pay back the money if your business model does not work and you end up closing it down? Always put yourself into the position of the person being asked, too. It will help you cover questions and concerns.

The Response to Your Proposal

Then comes the moment of truth. The lender responds to your loan proposal.

The person receiving your loan proposal can respond in one of three ways. They can:

Approve your proposed loan terms and accept all your terms. Congratulations! You did a great job explaining what your plans.

Suggests alternative loan terms: your lender likes your plan, but doesn't accept your terms. The lender or investor will make alternative suggestions for the terms of the investment or loan. It is up to you to respond. If you did your homework well, you already have a plan B with different terms (better terms for the investor or lender). Don't feel offended if you asked to provide different terms. You still did very well and you are almost there.

Rejects your loan proposal: If this occurs, you should try to find out why they rejected the loan proposal. If it makes sense, you can present a modified proposal that contains different loan terms at a later time. But, to be honest, in 99% of these cases, you are better off asking somebody else or coming up with a complete different way of funding your business with venture capital.

As previously mentioned in a different topic, the SBA provides help and funding. Talk to them. It does not cost you anything to talk to somebody who is there to help.

The Business Plan

A business plan defines your business, identifies your goals, and serves as your company's resume. The main components include a current and future (pro forma) balance sheet, a current income statement, and a cash flow analysis of your business. This will help you to allocate business resources properly, to handle unforeseen events, and to make good, solid business decisions. Because the business plan provides specific and detailed information about your company and (as an example) how you will repay a loan, a good business plan will be a crucial part of any loan application to a bank. Additionally, it will inform your sales personnel, your suppliers, and other third parties about your operations and business goals.

The importance of a comprehensive, detailed business plan can't be overemphasized. Many important things depend on it: external funding, credit lines from suppliers, management of your operations and finances, promotion and marketing of your business, and finally achievement of your goals and business objectives.

If you are tempted to start a business without having a business plan, you will very likely have trouble running a successful operation. A business plan is like the blue print of your business. Imagine a builder building your new house without having a blue print. Writing these things down is not most enjoyable thing for a new business owner to do. Make sure to put in the time and research into creating a solid business plan.

The Important Questions

Before you begin writing your business plan, consider four important questions:

- What service or product does your business provide and what needs does it try to fill?

- How will you attract customers?

- Who are the potential customers for your products and/or services and why should they purchase it from you?

- Where will you get the financial resources (cash, loan, etc.) to start your business?

A business plan usually has the following sections:

- Cover sheet

- Statement of purpose

- Table of contents

- Business operations which includes the following:

  A. A description of your business

  B. Your marketing strategy and plan

  C. Your competition

  D. Operating procedures

  E. Personnel / staff

  F. Business insurance

- The financial data pertaining to your business which can include:

A. Loan applications

B. Capital equipment and supply list

C. Balance sheet

D. Break-even analysis

E. Pro-forma income projections (profit and loss statements)

- Three-year summary

- Details by month, first year

- Details by quarters, second and third years

- Assumptions upon which projections were based

F. Pro-forma cash flow

Additional documents can include:

- Tax returns of principals for last three years

- Personal financial statement (available at your local bank)

- For franchised businesses, a copy of the franchise contracts and all supporting documents provided by the franchisor

- Copies of letters of intent from suppliers, etc. (if available)

- Copy of proposed lease contract or purchase agreement / contract for office space

- Copy of all business licenses and other legal documents (if related to the business)

- Copy of resumes of all principals / company officers

If you start a new business and do not have financial data going three years back, you can substitute this with solid statements of your current situation. Described above is the ideal case. Adjustments need to be made if necessary. Be detailed. It'll be to your own advantage. Ask your bank so that you can work with their small business specialists. Regular tellers might be friendly, but you want to make sure that you get accurate information.

What Makes a Good Business Plan?

Is it the length of a business plan? The information it contains? How well it is written, or the brilliance and excellence of the strategy it describes? No.

A business plan will be very difficult to execute unless it is simple, very detailed, realistic and complete. Even if the business plan has all the items listed, a good business plan will need someone to follow up with and check on it, too. The plan also depends on the human elements it's built on, particularly the aspects of commitment and involvement.

The first step in successfully implementing a business plan into your business is to have a good business plan. There are also several other elements that will make your business plan more likely to be successfully implemented.

Is the plan simple and easy to understand and to act on? Does it communicate its contents easily and practically and does it make sense?

Is the plan specific and detailed? Are its objectives concrete and measurable? Is the plan realistic? Are the sales goals, the expense budget, and milestone dates realistic? Nothing prevents implementation more than unrealistic business goals. Can you achieve the goals you have set?

Is the plan complete at all? Does it include all the necessary elements to be successful? The requirements for a business plan may vary depending on the actual context. There is no guarantee that the plan will work as conceived if it doesn't cover the main issues.

The process of preparing the business plan has to include an organized, logical view of all of the important aspects of a business. Don't use a business plan to show how much you know yourself about your business. Nobody will read a long-winded, overly-detailed business plan: neither your bank nor venture capitalists. Years ago, people were favorably impressed by long business plans. Today, nobody is interested in a business plan that is more than 40 or 50 pages long. Don't waste your time and the time of others by writing a book. Write a business plan that impresses and is to the point.

Do i Need a Business Plan If I'm Not Seeking Financing?

In order for your small business to succeed, you need to know where you're going and how you'll get there. Creating a business plan forces you to set your own goals, determine the resources you will need to execute your business plan, and to foresee problems that might otherwise broadside you and would prevent you from being successful.

If your business plan is not being used to solicit funding you can create an informal plan only, one that serves primarily as a planning tool for yourself to keep you on track. An informal plan can also be shown to potential business associates and partners.

How Do Investors and Bankers Read a Business Plan, and What Do They Look For?

Don't expect every person to give your business plan a thorough read through. In fact, you really can only count on them to skim it. Investors and bankers know what they're looking for in a business plan. They want to see a business that will grow rapidly and someday return a handsome profit. Bankers want to see a business that will be able to pay off the loan they are granting. Venture capital firms, for example, expect to receive an average of five times their original investment within five to seven years.

Keep in mind that investors rarely put money into a "product". They invest in a business. Many great products have floundered because the inventors did not understand how to get people to buy them. So be sure to show that you understand how to market your product or service. If your banker does not understand your business model, he will not grant you the loan you are looking for.

How Long Should My Business Plan Be?

30-40 pages should suffice. Anything longer than that and you risk alienating a potential investor, or you force them to skim through the document rather than read it. You won't be impressing anyone by creating a 200-page document. What's contained in the plan is much more important than how long it is. The more concise, detailed, and readable your business plan is, the more focused your business will appear. Focus on those details that tell the story of your business, that set you apart from your competition, that make your business appear to be a good, solid financial investment, and that show you will be profitable.

Is a Business Plan Helpful in this Fast-Paced World?

A well written and researched business plan will not only prepare your company for today's business and market conditions but tomorrow's unforeseen events. All business plans should have a contingency section to accommodate for the future. Your business plan is a plan that will not just sit on the shelf for 12 months but will always be updated when new market conditions or strategic changes take place. Plan your changes thoroughly. Running a business requires patience. Making changes too often and to quickly might result in your business going down faster than you can re-write your business plan.

Do the Readers Need to Sign a Non-Disclosure Agreement?

A non-disclosure agreement can raise red flags with your intended audience. A seasoned banker or investor is bound by client confidentiality and may find a NDA insulting. Secondly, if the business needs to protect its ideas and concepts at this stage of the game than there may not be any barriers for others to enter the market. A simple confidentiality clause at the front of the plan should suffice. If you are selling your business or if you are seeking a strategic alliance/partnership, a non-disclosure may be necessary. If in doubt, consult your lawyer.

Doing Business

Running a business requires many skills and a lot of knowledge and experience. If you are just starting out, you will quickly need to make up for any lack of knowledge and experience before it hurts the success of your business.

The following sections will give you a good idea of what is required to run a business.

Web Hosting Companies – The Competition

The Web hosting industry is extremely driven by competition. There are thousands (maybe tens of thousands) of small and large Web hosting companies out there. It is nearly impossible to stay current when researching this industry. Web hosts shut down, and at the same time, two others open the doors for business. A printed directory would be outdated one hour after being published. There are probably as many good Web hosts out there as there are bad ones, but you mainly hear stories about the bad ones. And there are no guarantees that a Web host who is considered to be good will offer the same quality of service two years down the road.

What kind of companies are out there? What is your competition like if you are a Web host? What do you look for if you are a customer looking for a Web host? The following part of the book will describe the most common types of Web hosting companies out there.

The kid Shop

One of the bad things with doing business online is that it is nearly impossible to know who you are really dealing with. It could be your own grandma running a server from her room in the retirement home or it could be a 13 year-old kid who runs a small business out of his or her room on a DSL connection. However, you will notice if you are dealing with a professional Web host or with a kid when it comes down to things like service and customer support in critical situations. If things go smooth, you won't really see the difference unless the technology (server, bandwidth, performance, etc.) is already horrible and it is obvious that there is something wrong. A kid shop usually won't offer a regular way to accept payments via credit card. If at all. PayPal is as good as it gets. Not that PayPal is a bad way for accepting credit card payments, but if it is the only option other than checks or cash, it should ring a bell and warning flags should go up. There is also no real business phone available and the business address sounds more like a residential address and not a business address. If there is a phone number and you suspect dealing with a kid shop, call them up during normal school hours or late at night and check who answers the phone.

The business name could be another indicator. Most professional Web hosting companies are run as an LLC or as a corporation. If the business Web page does not indicate that it is an incorporated company or an LLC, I would ask questions. You can also research this by looking up the information in public registers with the city or state where the business is located. Please be aware. It is usually a combination of things that points out that you are eventually dealing with a Web hosting company run by a kid.

Of course there will always be excepts to the rule. I have seen teenagers being more successful doing business than adults.

The 'Gone Tomorrow' Shop

Some Web hosting companies are not run very professional. The owner does not really have a sense for business and economics. The math they do when starting the business only looks at immediate profit. But that is not the way to run a business. They match any price out there, no matter how low the price is. They know they pay $55.00 for 50 GB bandwidth in wholesale and they know that they can oversell the capacity by at least four (4), often even more than that. That means they actually sell 200 GB bandwidth on a 50 GB package. This "over-selling" is very common in the industry and will be explained later on at this Web site. The problem with this type of Web host is that they are usually not prepared to expand their capacity and are not prepared to provide good customer service to all their clients. All they are interested in is the profit they can make, no matter what. They also do not work with a business plan and/or a budget. They do not calculate their real cost of doing business. All they see is the profit they can make. Again, they will beat any price of their competition. When it comes down to support and time needed to support the clients, they basically work for pennies. They offer annual hosting for $10.00 with a one-time payment. How do they intend to cover the cost of support with those prices?! When the going gets tough, these kind of Web hosts simply get going. They close their doors and leave their customers out in the rain.

How do you identify this kind of host? This is pretty easy. Just look for the cheapest Web hosts out there. And do the math yourself.

The Web host sells you a hosting package for 5 GB bandwidth (monthly) and 200 MB of disk space for $30.00 per year.

Assuming an rate of $5.25 (you have to put a value on your own work, right?!) for an hour of work and 15 minutes of support time (including invoicing and billing) per customer per month (some need more, some need less. This is just an average). This adds up to three hours of support per customer per year. So, the Web host wants to be paid $5.25 per hour, three hours of support a year per customer equals $15.75 per year. This leaves $14.25 from the $30.00 annual hosting fees.

Now the Web host needs to pay fees for collecting the payment (for example, credit card fees). In our case, we will assume this to be a $0.50 one-time fee. This leaves $13.75 leftover from the original $30.00 per year.

Now let us assume that the client only uses one GB of bandwidth of the purchased 5 GB bandwidth per month and that 1 GB is what the Web host has put into consideration for his calculation. Assuming the Web host can purchase this 1 GB for $0.75 per month, this would add up to $9.00 per year, effectively leaving us with $4.75 of the original $30.00.

We haven't covered any of the other costs of doing business yet. But at this point we just go and play with the numbers a little bit to demonstrate why and how this business model will fail.

A) Let's assume the customer actually uses 4 GB bandwidth per month out of the five he has purchased. This would add an additional $27.00 to the costs in our calculation.

B) Assuming the customer needs one hour of support per month. How is the Web host being paid for this or can he afford to pay for support when only charging $30.00 per year? So, you figure out very easily what the quality of this hosting provider is.

The Solid Host
There are many small to medium-size Web hosting providers out there who charge fair prices and deliver good value in return. Pricing is affordable but not the cheapest. Support requests are handled very professionally and relatively quickly. These hosts do not necessarily do lots of advertising. They live from word of mouth advertising and networking in many cases. They might offer a trial account or a money back guarantee for up to 30 days so that the new customer can test drive the offer. All critical information about server hardware, the data center, and the business location is easy to find on the Web site and very often

you can even find a phone number. Support is usually done through the Web site or via e-mail. I have even seen a Web host shut down the sign-up page and discuss the issue of growth with his clients. You know you have found a good Web host if something like this happens. If the host targets international clients from all over the world, support is usually available 24/7. Other hosts that only target the local market or perhaps the national market might not offer tech support around the clock. In most cases, this is not a problem at all. These hosts work when their customers work. Solid Web hosts may also offer dedicated servers and other technologies to their clients, too. It really depends on the actual size of the business and what the target market is.

The Solid Host – Gone Bad
If some businesses reach a certain size, you may see a change. I don't know if the business owners go crazy or what, but I am always amazed how a good company with a good reputation can go from good to bad. Support goes down the drain. Problems that are highly visible are denied and not resolved. The staff has a high turnover rate and/or the operation is under-staffed period. I assume that the high level of cash coming in has to do with this. Some people are just not able to handle large sums of money. They might mix businesses expenses with personal stuff or just become greedy. They lose their sense for doing business carefully and no longer act responsibly. In many cases, this is a slow process and not immediately visible.

How do you identify this kind of a Web host? First of all, there is no one single indicator. It is usually a sum of several issues that make up the situation. If your requests for support suddenly start taking much longer to be resolved, this could be one of these cases. The Web host denies problems like downtime and blames it on the customer instead or claims that there was no downtime at all. Your credit card gets charged twice in the same month and it is a drag to get a refund or to get the Web host to acknowledge the mistake at all.

The Large Host

The large host has its own data center. They usually employ a large number of staff and have 24/7 support available. Support usually comes through the Web site or by phone and is very professional. The technology is well-chosen and selected for reliability. They offer different solutions for many situations, including fail-over configurations for Web sites. This is not standard at normal Web hosts but as the larger hosts target mainly business clients, they also cover this part of the market. Pricing, in general, is higher compared to smaller operations but is justified by the way such operations are run. These hosts have a large advertising budget and can easily be found when conducting a search on the Internet. In most cases, an individual is better off with a smaller Web host if price is a consideration.

The ISP Web Host

Many Internet service providers offer free Web space to their clients as part of the deal. These are usually standard packages with no features at all or just a handful of basic features. Prices range from free to $$$ per month. There is no rule. The client does not need a domain name but uses a sub folder or sub domain under the ISP's domain name. I personally do not really consider this actual Web hosting. But many personal Web sites only exist because of the free Web space offered by ISPs. It's an affordable way to start out when you want to build a small Web site.

The Friend Host

In some cases a friend or a family member runs his or her own Web server and offers Web hosting to friends and family. Sometimes it is free, sometimes they charge a little money for it to reduce costs. These Web hosts can be the best or the worst deals a customer can get. No generic recommendation can be made. If you need to have a business Web site hosted and need reliable service and uptime, stay away. Don't be cheap.

The Web Designer Host

f you get your Web site made by a Web designer, they usually try to sell you the Web hosting as part of the deal. Web designers usually rent Web space or a server somewhere else and use it to sell this kind of service. Support is only available during business hours in these cases. If the client wants to move to a different Web host, it might be more difficult because of the nature of the business relationship. Some Web designers also make it more difficult for the client and try to block the move. They usually over-charge the client with their Web hosting anyway and try to defend these charges because of the actual service they provide. If you look closer at the work they do, you will see that in many cases there are no extra services provided. They just charge higher fees. Of course, there are exceptions to the rule but in 80% of the cases I have seen, the client could have saved a lot of money by moving to a cheaper Web host without losing quality of service. The Web designers take advantage of clients by making false statements or by not sharing all the details. The clients that are taken in by this ruse usually have not done any research on Web hosting options either.

Web Hosting Customers (Categorized)

What kind of clients can you expect when being a Web host?! When a new client signs up, you don't really know what to expect yet. All you have is that e-mail message with the domain name and the client data. Will it be an easy client who never needs support or will it be a nightmare for your support team?! Here is a look of what kind of customers you can actually expect as a Web host.

"I want it all for less"

Some people just don't care about quality. Everything they do, everything they get, has to be at least free or somebody has to give them money for it before they take it. When (if) those people really need something and they realize they have to pay for it, they just want the cheapest deal possible. All for less. If you get one of these clients, be prepared for the fact that these people do not want to pay fair value for your services but they will still expect full service at it best. As soon as they see a better deal somewhere else, they pack their bags and move on. That one dollar that they will save over a period of one year seems to give them a special kick. If you don't give them what they want, they will not hesitate to make you look bad in public forums. They will complain in public to get what they want. A good Web host should try to steer clear of this kind of client.

"I don't know what I am doing"

These clients have no clue about Web hosting, but they think they know it all. Nobody has ever told them that they don't know anything about Web hosting (or they have been but didn't believe it). Be prepared to hold the hand of these customers. They will need a lot of attention and will submit helpdesk calls whenever they think something is wrong. They also like to play around with things they don't know to handle (those evil control panels ;-)). This can result in broken Web sites or scripts or anything related to Web hosting. In most cases, they accept help and are very thankful. They are good customers, but if you have a short fuse, you will know it quickly. You would prefer to have different customers. However, if you love to deal with people and have the right touch with these customers, you can build up a very solid and loyal customer base this way.

Joe Average

Joe is not new to Web hosting. He has a very good idea of what he wants and what he needs. He likes to experiment a little bit so you will have to pick up the pieces every once in while. He knows that good quality requires spending a little more money and he is willing to pay for it. He is usually on a budget and so he will choose neither the cheapest package nor the most expensive one. Once he is settled in with his Web site, things tend to be quiet for a while until he starts experimenting again and it starts all over.

The Pro

Pros are usually very knowledgeable. They came to you because they expect quality service and certain features for their Web hosting account. They will know when your server went down and expects you a) to fix it fast and b) to explain what happened. If your server platform is unstable, they will move on and perhaps tell others about your problems, if it is justified and true. If you can explain what happened and fix the problem, the pro can be very loyal and supporting. Things break, no matter how good the quality of the hardware or the service is. It depends on how professional you are in handling the situation. These kind of clients can be very rewarding because if you treat them right, they will bring you even more business.

"I don't know what I am doing II"

He knows he needs a Web site. He know he needs a domain name and a Web host. But that's all he knows. He found somebody who made him a Web site a while back, but he still needs a Web host. Money is usually not a problem. He would rather pay a little more to get the better service. If he has the choice between your budget plan and your top notch pro plan with 25 GB bandwidth, he will go for the big package. His site might only use 25 MB bandwidth a month, but he would rather have some spare resources available, even if it is overkill (but you never know).

The Spammer

The spammer comes with a stolen credit card and either a fake or strange looking domain name. He only needs the account for a few days. As soon as you send him the account data, he will upload his SPAM script and files and then start sending out SPAM until you shut him down. These people suck and make your life more difficult. The only protection is increased fraud filtering, common sense and monitoring.

The invisible client

Invisible clients pay for their account, upload their Web sites and then you never hear from them again. The monthly fee is always there on time because they always pay. Sometimes you're tempted to call them or e-mail them to see if they are still alive (but you don't or do you?!). The invisible client uses less than half of their allotted resources, if at all. These are the perfect clients and you wish everyone were like this.

These are the main customer groups I have observed in the Web hosting industry. There are a few others but most of your clients will fit into one of the categories listed above.

Customer Loyalty

Loyal customers are the foundation of almost every business. Going the extra mile to provide outstanding customer service is the first step to customer loyalty. But there is more. Of course, your products and services in general need to be good. If you offer lousy uptime there is no real reason for your customers to be loyal. If you don't deliver, you don't deserve loyalty - period.

Here are a few suggestions gaining customer loyalty.

Be Smart

Be smarter than your customers are. Make sure you and your staff always (no exceptions) have more answers than your customers have questions. Most people are very loyal to expertise and proven skills.

Pay Attention

Pay attention to what your customers really want from you and what they really are hoping to find. If you see a pattern, follow it and adjust accordingly.

Attitude and Outfit

Show a positive attitude. Always be on time; never ever run late when a customer is involved. Be professional, act professional. If you meet with a customer, don't look like you are coming from a .COM company (even if you are) where shorts and T-Shirts are business attire. Don't over-dress either.

Dump Strict Policies

Don't make customers think that doing business with you is a risk. Be generous and flexible. Every situation is unique, and your decisions should be, too. If a customer is not satisfied, give him his money back and try spinning this into an even bigger sale.

Don't Hire Unlikable People

Nobody likes to give money to someone they don't like. Even if your staff might never really talk to customers and only communicates via e-mail or forums, personality will always shine through. After a while, a customer will sense who he is dealing with.

Don't Be Pushy

Don't try to push a customer into something they don't want, they don't need or they are not sure about. Provide options, be patient. Customers like that more than a stupid sales pitch.

Offer Superior Products

Add a little more to each product or service than necessary.

None of these things alone with buy you loyal customers, but a combination of things will make it very difficult for a customer to leave. If you get a customer to this point, you are able to ask for a higher price for your products and most of them will be happy to pay a little more so that they can continue to enjoy the service and the products that you provide.

Pricing Strategies

When starting as a Web host, you will need to decide on a pricing strategy. To develop a good pricing structure, you will need to know what your target market is. Just throwing a couple of hosting plans out onto your Web site won't cut it.

Find out what your cost for providing hosting services really is. How much does a GB of bandwidth cost you wholesale and how much do you pay for disk space? These are the main factors for creating a basic price structure. Once you have that information, you will need to put a price on your services and support. You don't want to give your work away for free. So, it has to be worth something, right?!

With all this information at your disposal, you can go and setup a pricing structure and start your business. But wait! That is not everything yet. What about your target group of customers? If you target the lower end of the market, you can't simply place your pricing in the upper range of Web hosting. You need to decide whether you would prefer 100 customers paying $5.99 a month (=$599.00) or whether you would prefer having only 50 customers who instead pay $11.99 per month (=$599.50) for the same package. It might be easier to find 100 customers who want to pay no more than $5.99 per month for Web hosting, but you have to take into consideration the fact that you will also then have to support 100 customers. You need to bill 100 customers and you will need to expect 100 support requests to come in. You will need to set up 100 accounts and you will need to monitor these 100 accounts for spammers or someone doing illegal stuff using your hosting service.

If you decide to go with a higher pricing structure, it might take a little longer to get customers (not everyone is willing to pay $11.99 for Web hosting), but from what I have described above, you know you will have to do less work to get the same money. In the long run, you will also be able to support more clients and still increase your income, compared to a pricing structure with lower prices. At one point, you would need to hire somebody to help you out with all the support requests. This will put a dent into your flow of income for a while until you have caught with new sign-ups.

Marketing and Reputation

The next issue is marketing and reputation. If you go into a dollar store to buy something, you know that everything is dirt cheap. You do not expect the highest quality either; you know it is cheap stuff. The same is true for Web hosting. If you compare Web hosting providers, you will see Web hosts with the lowest pricing on earth and you will see others with much higher prices. Both options get your Web site on the Internet, but do they provide the same kind of service? Probably not. That does not mean the most expensive Web host is the best option, but if somebody can make a living charging that much more for the same kind of service, customers expect this host to be of higher quality. So in your case, this means that you do not want to be the cheapest Web host around because people will question the quality of your service. But if you start with your prices too high, it will take forever to get clients. Start somewhere in the middle (lower part of the range) and then slowly increase pricing over time once your business has its name out on the street and once you have built a good reputation. Of course, if your target group is the lower end of the market, go for it and see if it works for you.

Neither of the two strategies is 100% wrong or right. You just need to figure out which one fits your business model best.

Staff and Salary

Sooner or later, the time will arrive when you have to hire somebody to help you. You will need to prepare a couple of things before posting a "Help wanted" ad on your Web site or in the local newspaper.

Job Description

Take some time and create a detailed job description, not for the ad but for yourself. Think about everything you want the employee to do. The duties and requirements of the position needed to be laid out properly. This will give you a good impression of what you can expect from the future team member. It will also give the employee an idea of what is expected of him or her. One of the biggest mistakes made when hiring employees are allowing different expectations on both side because of an inadequate job description. Avoid these mistakes by doing your homework, and do it before you hire.

Contractor or Employee

You also need to decide if you want a contractor or a real employee to join your team. Both options offer advantages and disadvantages. If the contractor isn't operating as a company, you will want him to fill out the IRS 1099 form. The contractor is responsible for paying his own taxes, not you. Employees get a W2 form at the end of each year instead to report their income. You are responsible for deducting taxes from the employee's paycheck and sending it to the IRS. You are most likely also responsible for paying for the social security, workers comp, and unemployment. Check with an account or lawyer and perhaps consider hiring a payroll company to take care of everything for you. Other things to consider are:

- Term of contract (open or limited time, for example, three months)

- Employee benefits (health insurance, etc.)

- Job requirements / responsibilities

- Probationary period

- NDA / non compete clause (check with a lawyer to make sure it is legal in the area you live in)

The Contract

You will need a very clear and detailed contract that specifies what is required from the employee and what is expected from you. The contract should list everything that might need to be regulated this way. Check with a lawyer and also do your homework. Every state has different requirements. Your local SBA office should be able to help you. http://www.nolo.com has also some very good information available. The whole topic is very complicated if you have never done it before. Be safe and take your time and hire a professional (personnel or outsource) to avoid mistakes.

Besides all the legal stuff, you also have to make up your mind about what you can pay your employee. The Web hosting industry has different models in use right now. For support technicians the pay can either be per ticket or salary-based. Or it can be a combination of both. If you pay your staff per ticket, you will also come up with a scheme for easy tickets (less work) and for more difficult tickets (more time consuming). Our research has shown prices per ticket ranging from $1.25 to $2.50 per ticket. You can also add incentives for tickets answered within a certain time after the customer has submitted the ticket. As faster the tickets are answered, the better your company looks to the customer. Speedy customer service is a definite plus. You will need to put into consideration where the employee will be located. Somebody in a rural area has fewer costs of living compared to somebody living in New York City, for example. If you want to keep good employees, you need to make sure that the salary is adequate and fair. You could offer frequent pay increases to motivate the employee or contractor to do better work.

If you need to hire a system administrator, you will look at a higher cost. Depending on how much help you need, you should perhaps start out hiring somebody by the hour. This will keep your costs low and gives you time to see how the admin performs. If you find a good administrator and your finances allow hiring him, it might be a step to consider. Highly skilled and motivated employees are worth their money. Your business reputation will depend on those people, too. Selecting the right staff is important. Salary pay per hour for administrators can range from \$20.00/per hour to \$90.00 per hour. Perhaps a service contract will be an option for the beginning. This will give you a certain amount of the administrator's time at a fixed cost.

Motivation
Motivate your employees. A small bonus here, or an Amazon.com gift certificate there, will do a lot to keep the employee motivated. Research has shown that these small motivational things are much better for your business than the one-time raise a year. If your employees work in an office location, have a Pizza Day once a month/week and perhaps offer free beverages (coffee, juice, Coke, Mountain Dew, and Sprite, etc.).

The Hiring Process
Once you start receiving the resumes, make sure you take the time to read them carefully. There are several different approaches for this and you will need to figure out which one works best for you. You can sort the resumes by level of experience. Newbies might not have experience, but they might be much more motivated and willing to learn. They also ask for less money. But they might leave your company soon once they have some experience under their belt. Now they are able to make more money somewhere else. More seasoned applicants need less supervision and less training. The return of investment (the salary) for you is probably higher but at a price (higher salary). Make sure you ask for references and check them, too.

Hiring is one of the toughest elements of small business management. Determining what talent a business needs to succeed, then finding the time and know-how to recruit these people is a real problem for many entrepreneurs. Successful hiring can be expensive and time consuming. Unsuccessful hiring can be disastrous for your company's health.

Markets so change. The information provided here might not match the market and location where you are located. Do thorough research and don't be shy hiring professional help for this important step.

How to Fire an Employee

One of the most difficult tasks you will face as a business owner will be firing employees. Employees who consistently break the rules, do not perform the functions of their job, or cause difficulties for your business can not only be a strain on the work environment and your cash flow, but it can also hinder your business from thriving and performing as expected. This tutorial will give you steps and hints about firing employees or associates.

Document, Document, Document

The first step in preparing to let go an employee is to make sure you have all the documentation you need. When you give verbal warnings, be sure to document them properly. Make a case for this specific situation by documenting everything you did before making the decision of releasing the employee. This includes anything that shows that you tried to solve problems and make them better. Your business should have a well documented procedure for what it expects from employees and anything that is considered grounds for immediate dismissal. Be sure to use these as guidelines and consult with a lawyer experienced in HR questions if necessary.

Witnesses

Have a friend, family member, or business partner be there to assist in any paperwork and issues that come from the employee. Not only does this representative help with anything you might forget, he or she also serves as a witness if a lawsuit arises. This will be difficult for both of you but in the end, it will be well worth the effort.

"I've been fired, but why?"

Explain to the employee the performance you have expected, the steps you have taken to help them achieve that performance, and that he/she has not met them. Do not say more than you have to, just state why they are being dismissed and fill out any exit paperwork. If you are upset, cool down before talking to them. If you have to fire somebody over the phone because he or she is in a different location, advise the employee that you have somebody with you listening to the conversation. Make it very clear that you are in control and prepared.

Establish Exit Procedures
Make sure you backup any important files before firing the employee and take steps to lock this person out of all the computer systems. Change all the passwords but make sure the employee does not realize that before the actual moment of truth. It is also recommended that you fire someone on a Monday and not on a Friday. Employees fired on Fridays have the whole weekend to stew, while those fired on Mondays usually are more upbeat because they have the week ahead of them. Be sure to explain when the last paycheck is coming, when benefits terminate, and any information regarding extending their health coverage or any other details (if applicable).

Remember to keep the meeting short and to the point. Explain to the other team members that you fired the individual without going into too many details. They do not need to know all the details, but you need to make sure that they understand that this was not a personal dispute between you and the employee fired. You want your employees to be honest when disagreeing on something and not be scared about getting fired. When a new potential employer calls you for a reference, remember to just state the title and dates of employment. Specify that you are not able to provide any further information. Advise your remaining employees that your business policies specify that all calls for references have to go through HR (you?) or yourself. Document again how the complete process of firing went, what the employee had to say and anything else that happened.

Checking Out Your Competition

Your business may already be well established and is thriving. New customers sign up frequently and everyone is happy.

However, you are not the only one doing Web hosting and the competition is tough. If you want to get ahead and stay ahead, you must keep abreast of what's going on in the Web hosting industry. In order to compete within your market areas, you have to know what your competition is doing and what the market is demanding. This means looking at your competitors Web sites from time-to-time and see what they are doing (Web hosting businesses do almost all their business online).

The Internet makes this an easy task. In another business, for instance, you would have to take real effort to find out what the competition is doing. You would have to call your competitor and pretend to be a customer or even go there and buy something or spend some time in the store as an example. As a Web host, you do not have to go that far. Get on the Internet and browse some Web sites.

Since you are an Internet business, it's easy to check out other business Web sites to see what's going on. "Google" (meaning: do a search on your competition via Google.com) the most common key words and see whose company comes up on top or shows up on the advertisement area. Anyone on page one and two of your search result did a good job because they have a high ranking.

So, check them out to see what else they are good with. I recommend visiting at least ten competitors' Web sites. Here are some of things to look for:

The Web Site Design Itself
After looking at several, are you seeing a new trend? Maybe everyone is starting to put audio clips on their Web site, or the

look is getting cleaner (or busier). You want to look current, if not on the cutting edge.

The Specials
What sort of specials are they offering? Are there any good deals or upgrades in their hosting packages?

Money-Back Guarantees
Are money-back guarantees prominently featured? Do they still last as long as the did the last time you looked at them?

Language
Are there new phrases that you need to take note of, like sticky taglines, buzz words or brilliant descriptions of boring old stuff?

Product Descriptions
How do they describe what they do or what they offer? Is there something you could learn from the way they describe their products?

Innovation
Has someone come up with a new line of products or new services – something no one in the industry has seen yet?

What you are doing is taking a lot at things from your potential customers' viewpoint. Today's smart consumer shops around before he signs up for Web hosting or registers a domain name. Consumers compare what is being offered and how, in order to make informed decisions.

So periodically take the trip your potential customers do. Visit your competition and see what it's like. You could be in for some surprises. Make sure to take some notes or even make screenshots for comparison when it is time for you to make your rounds again.

Also keep track of who is listed on the first two pages of your Google search. Newcomers might have discovered something that your business is lacking. I would recommend making these visits every three months.

Buying or Selling a Web Hosting Business

You might come to the point where you would like grow by acquiring another Web hosting business or maybe you want to sell your own business and retire from the industry. It is easy to find a buyer and it is also not difficult to find sellers who want to get out. But how do you put a fair value onto a Web hosting business? This part of the process is the most difficult step. The seller always wants the highest price while the buyer wants to pay a little as possible. The gap between those two expectations will either make or break a deal.

Here are a few consideration and recommendations about how to determine what a Web hosting business is worth and what people are willing to pay for clients.

The Worth of Clients

What are they worth at all (money-wise) when buying a Web hosting business? How do you determine their value? What do you have to keep in mind?

The first thing to consider and to find out about is what payment terms are in place for the clients? Do the clients pay monthly, quarterly, semi-annually, or even yearly? This is important to know since it will affect your cash flow right away. Imagine you pay for clients that have yearly payments in place. In the worst case you would have to work almost 12 months before seeing any money. Clients with yearly payments in place are worth much less to the buyer than clients who pay on a monthly basis. If a Web host has different payment models in place, you should split the clients into groups according to their payment schedule. Then work out a price for each group.

You also have to keep in mind that it is very often the case that clients do not like change. They will be leaving the new Web host very soon after the deal has been closed and the announcements to the clients have been made. From what I have seen, the percentage of this can go up to 15% in some cases, though 5% to 10% is a more likely. You should consider this when working out the deal.

Now it is time to determine how much the clients are worth! Common values put on clients in the Web hosting industry range from three to nine months of the monthly revenue. In some cases even up to 12 months revenue has been recorded. It really depends on the business model and the quality of the clients. Small business clients are less likely to leave the hosting company than a customer with a personal Web site.

The Brand Name

What else needs to be considered? If you are buying just the clients to integrate them into your business and under your business brand name, you'll be fine with the model introduced above. But what if you buy the complete business including the name? Building a brand is a difficult and time-consuming process. Buying an existing brand gives the buyer a short cut. The result is that the business brand name is worth quite a bit. How much is it worth? It depends on each single case.

One way to determine the value of a brand name is to see what the expected number of sign-ups per month is. Fifty new clients per month on average will give you a good ballpark number. Since it is more difficult to get new clients compared to keeping existing ones, the value put on these possible clients is less than the value put on existing clients. A three to six month value of the expected revenue from this seems to be a fair value for determining the brand name value. But again, this might vary and each case needs to be taken into consideration individually.

Assets

If a complete business is being sold, it might include hardware and software licenses. Determine the value of these items per age (especially hardware) and what kind of software licenses you would sell/buy.

Liabilities

Buying a business (not just the customer base) might also bring liabilities. Are there any employees to take onboard? Are there existing contracts with vendors (data center, software, etc.) that need to be fulfilled? Determine the outstanding monetary amount per item. Make sure that the supply cost is reasonable and that you are allowed to buy or sell the contract or agreement. Under normal circumstances, this should not pose a problem. But if the cost or contractual agreement is limiting how you take advantage of the business, this should be taken into consideration when making an offer for a business.

Terms

How about the terms of the payment when selling a Web hosting business? Paying for everything 100% is not a good thing. The seller walks away and you just have to hope that everything will go on as 'advertised'. A 60% payment when the deal closes gives the seller security to get his money. The buyer also knows that he is not risking 100% of his investment right away. The outstanding amount should be split into smaller payments. Depending on the overall amount of the outstanding money, the time frame for the payment should be split between 3 to 12 months before 100% are paid out. The smaller the amount is, the shorter the time frame should be.

A good way for the buyer to make sure he gets what he is paying for is to keep the seller around for three to six months. The contract should clearly state that the seller is available a certain amount of time or the outstanding price will not be paid. The seller should also sign a non-compete agreement and eventually a non-disclosure agreement to protect the buyer.

Strategy

Buying an existing business also requires good strategy upfront. Will you be integrating the clients into your business or run the new business under its old name? Do you want to move the clients to your hardware and consolidate or leave them where they are? How about support? Does your staff have the skills and knowledge to support the different environment? Do you have staff at all or do you eventually need to hire someone? Would you rather buy one big business or maybe many smaller ones? Consider these things when being in the market for buying a Web hosting business.

Mission Statement

Every organization or business has a mission, a purpose, a reason for being. The mission statement should be a clear and succinct representation of the company's purpose for existing. It should incorporate socially meaningful and measurable criteria addressing concepts such as the moral/ethical position of the company, the public image, the target market, products/services, the geographic domain and expectations of growth and profitability. At the very least, your organization's mission statement should answer three key questions:

- What principles or beliefs guide our work?

- What are the opportunities or needs that are the reasons we exist?

- What are we doing to address these needs and opportunities?

A mission statement should consist of one or two sentences and be a clear, concise statement of what the company is, what it does, for whom and where.

The intent of the mission statement should be the first consideration for any employee or business representative who is the position of evaluating any strategic decision. The statement can range from a very simple to a very complex set of ideas.

A mission statement can change over time. It does not have to be static. It is actually good to revisit your mission statement over time and adjust it to new developments in society, culture and business.

Examples
Here are some mission statements of other companies and organizations:

Mary Kay Cosmetics: "To give unlimited opportunity to women."

Food and Drug Administration: "The FDA is responsible for protecting the public health by assuring the safety, efficacy, and security of human and veterinary drugs, biological products, medical devices, our nation's food supply, cosmetics, and products that emit radiation. The FDA is also responsible for advancing the public health by helping to speed innovations that make medicines and foods more effective, safer, and more affordable; and helping the public get the accurate, science-based information they need to use medicines and foods to improve their health."

North Carolina - Secretary of State: "To serve and protect citizens, the business community and governmental agencies by facilitating business activities, by providing accurate and timely information and by preserving documents and records."

Sun Microsystems: "Solve complex network computing problems for governments, enterprises, and service providers"

Walt Disney: "To make people happy."

You can see from these different kinds of mission statements that most of the items mentioned above have been implemented in one way or the other. Make sure your business has a mission statement that you can identify with. Make sure your employees know the mission statement and understand the purpose of it.

Getting the Cash to Flow

You've already invested quite a bit of time, energy and your own money into getting your business set up. You may even already have customers. But customers don't do you much good if you aren't getting any money from them. Your customers are willing to pay but if you don't make it as easy as possible for them, there will not only be delays but headaches.

The easiest way and safest way to get your money is by letting your customers pay their fees to your credit card account. To let them do this, though, you need to have a credit card merchant account.

This chapter will help you get going in the right direction.

Selecting a Merchant Account

Shopping for a merchant account is a confusing and difficult process. And unfortunately, many merchants do themselves no big favor by going shopping without first understanding what they are really shopping for.

It's simply not enough to research the rates of banks and independent sales organizations/merchant account providers to find out which are lowest. You must also know the different types of accounts available to determine which one is really right for you. So why not just shop for the lowest rates?

Because the accounts that offer the cheapest rates won't necessarily be right for your business. Retail/card swiped accounts often have the lowest rates but carry requirements that, if not met by the merchant, will result in additional fees, surcharges, and even penalties. For example, if you're signed up for this type of account but are not able to swipe a card electronically, some processors charge you as much as one percent to two percent more. Being a Web host means doing business on the Internet. You might not even need to look at the rates for physical transactions. It is much more important to find out the rates for virtual transactions.

Let's go back to not being able to swipe a card electronically. In the business world, these are known as nonqualified or disqualified transactions. This means that the transaction won't meet all the requirements and therefore it doesn't qualify for the best rates. The real-world effect can be a monthly bill that's much larger than what you expected, leaving you wondering what happened to that great deal you thought you were getting when signing up with this provider. Always make sure you're using an account that's right for your business.

Crucial Distinctions

What kind of account types are there out there? This would be easy to answer if every merchant account provider used the same terms, fees, and structured pricing in the same way as everyone else. Unfortunately, life is never so easy. Nevertheless, please allow me to say that, in general, credit card merchant accounts are classified as one of the following account types:

Retail/card swiped accounts are designed with the typical brick-and-mortar merchant business in mind, one who can swipe the card through an electronic terminal reader as proof that the card was present.

Retail/keyed entry accounts are designed for situations in which the card is present but the merchant is unable to electronically swipe the card. The magnetic stripe might be damaged as an example. Important: The card numbers are keyed into the physical terminal.

Rates for these accounts are generally a little higher than those for card swiped accounts, but can be lower than Internet rates. Important: Retail/keyed entry merchant accounts require that the merchant can (not must) obtain a manual imprint of the card in addition to the customer's signature. Examples of merchants that fit this account type include mobile merchants, such as locksmiths and arts and crafts dealers. Why are the rates higher? Due to the higher risk somebody using a stolen credit card number and customer name to charge an account.

Mail order/telephone order/Internet accounts are for those merchants who don't usually see their customers and therefore cannot obtain a physical swipe read on a terminal or an imprint of the card. Not surprisingly, these transactions carry more risk and are therefore more expensive than normal rates. You will need a virtual terminal to be able to make keyed transactions. Authorize.net would be such a provider for a virtual terminal.

Which is Right for You?

Use a retail/card swiped account with a physical terminal if you actually see your customer and are able to electronically swipe 90 percent or more of your transactions. This is a good option for somebody doing local business from a physical store mainly selling non-recurring services.

Use a retail/keyed entry account if you always see your customer and can obtain a manual imprint of the card but not swipe it, or if you routinely swipe fewer than 90 percent of your sales. This sort of credit card merchant account is also a good option for a business mainly targeting the local market.

Use an Internet account anytime you don't see your customer face to face AND have a lot of recurring payments to take care of.

When doing the research, ask the merchant account provider to provide you with a sample invoice representing a typical month. Let them explain every single fee.

When is it Time to Get a Real Merchant Account?
In many cases, it makes sense to have your own merchant account when your monthly sales volume charged to credit cards reaches $1,000 or more. Close to that point the fixed fees for the merchant account equal the higher transaction fees or third party providers like Paysystems or 2Checkout.

How Does This Actually Work in the Web Hosting Industry?
Accepting credit card payments through your Web site actually requires multiple components. There are usually three things involved when a customer makes an online payment.

Your order form: the customer decides to use your services and accesses your order form on your Web site. You must have code/software in place that will collect the client information and billing information. The information must be stored in a way that it can be accepted by the payment gateway.

The payment gateway: this is the part that will transmit your customer's order information to an Internet merchant account provider (for example, Authorize.net). The payment gateway does the actual credit card processing in the moment the transaction happens.

The (Internet) merchant account: A credit card merchant account is an account with a financial institution (merchant account provider) or bank, which enables you to accept credit card payments from your clients. The payment gateway will transmit the billing information received when the actual transaction took place to the merchant account provider.

How Much Does a Credit Card Merchant Account Cost?

Understanding the total costs of your merchant provider can be tricky. Typically, an Internet merchant account will have several types of costs associated with it:

Application fees: Most merchant accounts will require an up-front application fee. This fee is supposedly to cover the initial costs for processing your application. In case you decide not to open a merchant account or if your credit standing is really bad, they still cover their initial costs. Although good providers waive these fees if they deny your application, I recommend that you choose a provider that does not require any up-front fees (if you can find one). Local banks might be a better option in that case. The fact that they want to keep their customers and you might move an account to another bank, often makes them do a little more.

On-going fixed fee: Almost every merchant account provider requires you to agree to a monthly fixed fee or "statement fee" as it is often named. This is simply another way to cover their fixed costs and to make money. It will be almost impossible to find a provider that does not require this type of fee on a monthly basis. However, do not choose a merchant account that requires you to pay more than $10.00 per month. In addition to that, most merchant providers require a minimum monthly fee (usually $20.00 or $25.00). This will bring your fixed fees to a minimum of $30.00/$35.00.

Discount rate: In most cases, the discount rate will be between 2% and 4%, depending on the card provider (Visa, AMEX, MasterCard/Diners Club/Discover). The discount rate is the sales commission the provider earns on each sale (but has to pass part of it on to their upstream provider, usually the credit card company). For example, if the discount rate offered is 3%, and you receive a sale through your Web site for $10, you will owe $0.30 to your credit card merchant provider.

Fixed transaction fee: Every credit card transaction will be associated with a fixed transaction fee. Usually the amount of the fixed transaction fee is between $0.20 and $0.30. Unlike the discount rate, the fixed transaction fee is the same for every transaction. Whether you get a $0.50 sale or a $100 sale, no matter if you have 10 transactions a month or 10,000 transactions, the fixed transaction fee will always be the same.

Termination Fees: Often hidden in the fine print of a contract, a termination fee can apply if you cancel your merchant account within a specified period of time (usually within one year). But beware; some credit card merchant account providers require a two-year commitment! Make sure you get this information upfront so that you can decide if you really want to sign a two year agreement.

Miscellaneous fees: There can be additional fees. Make sure you clearly ask for a list of all fees involved in writing from the provider. An example of a miscellaneous fee would be the charge back fee. If a client disputes a charge on a credit card you might get charged back. Not only will you lose the sale, you will also have to pay a penalty (charge back fee). Beware! Too many chargebacks on your account will lead to termination of your account by the provider.

Preventing Fraudulent Credit Card Transactions

Here are some of the possible indication of fraudulent transactions as experienced by Web hosting companies:

- The customer wants to pre-pay for a year.

- The domain name is registered for 5 years or more.

- Customers place orders using free e-mail providers like Hotmail, Yahoo, etc.

- The customer uses multiple cards to complete an order.

- The customer has an overseas address. AVS cannot validate international addresses.

- Multiple purchases are made in a short time period.

- The customer and billing addresses are different.

Security Features

AMEX, VISA, and MasterCard implement security features known as "CVV2" and "CVC2". These are the three-digit or four-digit numbers printed on the back side or front side (depending on the card company) of the card (signature panel) to the far right. The three/four-digit code helps to verify that the cardholder has the card in his possession. You can include the code in your transaction processing and require a match to successfully complete the transaction. If you are using a shopping cart for your hosting sign-up process, make sure that it is capable of collecting and processing these numbers. IMPORTANT: the ToS of the credit companies state that you are not allowed to store these numbers.

Address Verification Service

Use the Address Verification Service (AVS) on all US transactions to verify the billing information provided in the order with what is on file with the card issuing bank. As a bare minimum, the zip code should successfully match before the transaction is approved and you hand out the account information. You should retain the response information for some time in case of a chargeback.

Possible AVS messages include:

Y – Exact match on street address and 5 or 9 digit zip code.

A – Address matches, zip code does not .

Z – Zip code matches, address does not.

N – No match.

U – Address information is unavailable or issuer does not support AVS. These transactions are only applicable for Visa and the merchant isn't responsible for chargeback liability.

R – Issuer authorization system is unavailable, retry later.

E – Error in address data, unable to complete check.

G – Non-US Issuer not participating in AVS - Visa only. The error messages will vary from one provider to the next. Contact your provider for more information.

S – Address information is unavailable or issuer does not support AVS; MasterCard only.

The most important warning signs of fraudulent transactions are international orders. It is very sad to be so generic with this statement but the percentage of fraudulent orders goes up immediately if the order comes from a non-US location. Be aware of cities or countries with high rates of fraudulent transactions.

Malaysia, Indonesia, and most countries in the former Soviet Union tend to be source of many fraudulent orders.

Just Call Them

The most effective way to help eliminate fraud or chargebacks is to simply call the customer. A confirmation over the phone is most definitely advised for any large transactions. If you process a fraudulent transaction, not only do you lose the funds, but the product/service as well. A phone call, even if it is international, will save you a lot of hassle in the long run.

Suspicious?

What if you are suspicious of a transaction ? Contact your authorization center and let them know you are concerned about the transaction. They will look at the transaction and may give you advice. You should also call the customer to request additional information (copy of drivers license or passport as an example). Check the IP address of the sign-up and see where it is globally. Does it match the customer's address at least by country? Send a confirmation e-mail message to the customer verifying their order.

It may be a good policy to only accept orders with identical customer and billing addresses.

International Orders

You may want to be very picky about international orders since your protection against this type of fraud is very minimal and not accepting them could save your Web hosting business a lot of money.

Scarecrows

Placing fraud notices, buttons and images on your Web site and order forms will help discourage any person trying to place a fraudulent order. Make sure that the customer can see upfront that you are recording the IP address and that you will notify law enforcement agencies if necessary. It might not protect you in every case but eventually it will help cut down the number of fraudulent orders.

How to Compete Against the Big Guys

Many of the big Web hosting companies have a reputation for being invulnerable, but in fact it's very possible to compete against the Yahoos and 1&1s and still win.

The key to be successful is to remember that these big companies are not a one-unit business, but rather are made up of many business units (Yahoo: Search engine, Web directory, Web hosting, e-mail, advertising, and, and, and). Some of those business units are highly effective, others are more vulnerable to competition.

Let's take Microsoft for example. One company that successfully competes against Microsoft is Logitech, which competes by focusing on technology that Microsoft doesn't consider strategic, that is, computer accessories.

Logitech's strategy: remember Microsoft is a software and tools company, but it also used to dominate the mouse and keyboard market. Microsoft then started producing gaming equipment, such as joysticks, and steering wheels. It even sold speakers. It made great products but it did not become market leader in these areas and never made the final push against the competition like it did with Netscape.

Microsoft pulled back into the mice and keyboard markets after becoming to spread out and after loosing focus. Logitech continued to offer a broader range of products which could be combined with each other in retail packages (wireless mouse and keyboard). Although Microsoft continued to build quality products, Logitech started dominating this segment with a broad line of accessories including mice, keyboards, cameras, and speakers, all of great quality.

Logitech was able to grow to become market leader because they don't go around pointing out that they are beating the crap out of Microsoft. Executives often want to brag about beating the crap out of Microsoft, but it only motivates Microsoft to want to squash the competition. They stayed silent in the background and concentrated on making great products and marketing them. They stayed very focused. Microsoft has to watch markets that are much more strategic than peripheral hardware, but Logitech can fully concentrate on this one segment of the market.

This is one of the best ways to go after a dominant company. Find the areas where the giant isn't focused enough, and quietly slip in from behind and start taking market share. Inside the big and dominant company, the business unit you compete with will see declining revenues over time. It's not a large decline in a short period. Employees won't want jobs in that business unit. But once they are there, they'll either be treading water or looking to get out. Once the sleeping giant realizes that you have taken over a large share of that specific market, it might start acting against you, but if you play your cards right, you have a great position to fight back and to keep your share of the market. Or the sleeping giant just stays where it is and holds on to the market share that it has. No retreat but also no attack. It depends on how important that market share is in the strategic planning. The third option might be that the giant gives up this market segment and concentrates on its strategically important products. For example, not too long ago Microsoft stopped offering broadband products like wireless routers. It had a great product but the competition did not have to concentrate that much on other products and was (is) more focused.

Using the same tactics Microsoft used 10-15 years ago, Logitech has been able to establish itself as a market leader in the accessories segment. A job well done!

Large competitors often have two big weaknesses:

1). They often have an image problem which they refuse to even acknowledge. As a result, the leaders and upper management lose contact with their normal customers often forgetting that this is often the customer segment that made them big.

2). Large businesses also toss people into jobs without properly matching skills and position. Like many big companies, they have executives leading core units who took the job without formal training. People get the title of a CEO, and they start acting as if that instantly makes them an super manager, when in fact they simply don't know what they are doing. This can be a real problem for a business, especially during times of extensive growth. The Web hosting industry has many folks employed who have great technical knowledge, but when it comes down to having proper business skills, their business hits a big bump.

Large companies are very vulnerable to competition from a small, but smart company that goes after a certain market segment. Strategies for successful competition against large hosting Web hosting businesses include finding a market that they consider non-strategic, and you can even partner with the competition in areas where the companies don't compete. You can play against the giant without getting crushed.

More about beating the big guns

Many small business startups fail within the first 2 years of existence. There are several different factors reason for the failure. One reason many entrepreneurs often under estimate the need to find a niche market and to serve it well. Instead of finding the niche market they attack the big guys head on. If you have enough money to throw at 'this problem' you might succeed, but in reality almost every small business doing this will fail and eventually shutdown operations.

So, what should small business startups do to avoid this big mistake? How can they survive and grow and become successful?

As mentioned before - finding a niche market is the first big key to not be destroyed head-on buy the big guns. Never, ever try to be the "Wal-Mart" for everyone. Not everyone is your target group. Carve out a niche market, then slowly steal away market share from the market players. Eventually pick a niche that you know of where the market leader is not spending enough attention on. Grow here and grab market share. Eventually you will grow big enough without being noticed to become the market leader for this niche. Companies like Microsoft and Wal-Mart tend be slow moving but they have enough cash to catch up quick. We have seen situations where the small business owner was able to cash out big time from a situation where he/she was able to grab enough market share to be considered 'armed and dangerous' for the big guns.

Compete on things where large market players fall short. Compete on experience and value added services - not price. You will not be able to compete on price with somebody like Wal-Mart or Target. Their buying power is just too big for you to swallow. Let your experience disappear differences in price for a product. Give the customer the feeling that you know what you are talking about and that this experience is worth spending a little extra.

Emotions can be a big advantage for the small business startup. Bond with the clients and vendors. A personal (business) relationship that makes everyone feel good will get you repeat business and fair deals from vendors (friends don't steal from friends). If the vendor can make his share of revenue and you can get your share of the pot - everyone will be happy. Nobody likes to be squeezed by the big sales department of the market leader.

The work place. Be hands-on. Be the boss, but at the same time be the employee who does actual work. Don't get disconnected from your own business now that 'you are a the boss'. Stay involved as long as you can. Work harder than your employees do. Be emotional and inspire your employees with your dedication. The spark will eventually jump over and the productivity increase can be enormous. Make your work place 'cool'. Create an environment people want to work at. If employees wake up in the morning and really like to come to work because they enjoy what they do, you will definitely benefit from it. And keep in mind - you need all the help you can get when competing with the market leader. Be the employer of choice.

Be the star in your community. The place where you start your business can be the founding place of the next 'business empire'. People are proud if one of them makes it to the top. Remember Johnny Carson? He gave back to the community where he had grown up. Nobody outside of that local area really knew about it or had paid attention but the local population - they admired Johnny Carson and were thankful supporters. Keep this in mind when building a business. You might become as big as other market players, but doing well is not a matter of how many millions you have. On the other side - you do not want to build a business just to make $30K per year. Your goals should go much further out and higher. Try to be the best in your field. The sky is the limit.

Use technology. Technology can be your friend. Small businesses can respond much faster to market trends than the big guns. Be innovative. While you're the small guy you can use this to your advantage. Being small is no excuse when it comes to using sophisticated technology. See the advantages of what technology can do and put away with the whining about the next upgrade coming soon. As long as you calculate it properly and make your case, you can most likely provide a quick ROI (return on investment).

Of course many more things come into play in regards to business success. The steps outlined in this article however will give you a good head start when working on strategic placement of where and how your business should start. Good Luck.

The Reality of Self-Employment

Full-time Job + Hosting Business: Can it Be Done?

Y ou have made the decision to start your own business. Congratulations! But like it is for everyone else, it is difficult to make the jump. How are you going to pay your bills? How do you pay for food and the mortgage? Not many new entrepreneurs have enough funds to quit their job and start a new business from scratch. You will not know when the new business will generate enough income to pay your bills (if at all).

The most preferred solution would be to be able to continue working at your current job and at the same time build up your business. That way, you still have income but can also generate income from your new business. You're not the first one in this situation and you won't be the last. How did other people do it when they started?

It is very important during the startup time to be available to your customers. If your current job does not allow you to access the Internet and your own e-mail, it will be very difficult to start. Asking your boss for permission is usually not an option. If he knows you're leaving .....! You will also need to be careful not to abandon your tasks and duties of your job. Remember, one day you could be the employer and you sure don't want your employees to run down your business because they are concentrated on doing their own gig. So, maintain a high work ethic, even if it is hard and difficult. If you are able to use the Internet at work for your own things, be fair enough to do your job. You are still getting a salary from your employer.

So, what can you do to get your business going and still work for your existing employer? Try to automate things. Automation makes it look like that you are actually out there doing something, running your business. If you are selling domain names, automate it. There are plenty of scripts and software packages out there that will do this for you. Setup helpdesk software that includes a knowledge base. Fill the knowledge base with knowledge and how-to information. Reduce the chance of getting a helpdesk ticket for a simple question that wasn't answered in your knowledge base.

If you cannot access e-mail from work but if you have access to your corporate e-mail, use forwarders for your own e-mail and have messages forwarded to work. At least you will know what is going on and do not have to worry about open tickets or a new user signing-up. If worse comes to worst, you will be able to reply using your corporate e-mail (I still do not recommend doing this). Ask friends for help. If you know somebody who has Web access during the day while you are at work and is willing to help out, forward the message to him or her. Prepare those friends with e-mail templates and knowledge of what to do. A new account can be set up easily, maybe even via a script that your friend can execute with the information provided. You have to plan for these contingencies, though. Have some people you can trust lined up in case you need them. You could also check e-mail messages before you go to work. Visit a library at lunch for Internet access and check e-mail and work on tickets. As soon as you get home after work, dedicate some time to checking e-mail and working on tickets.

If you have the funds, buy a Pocket PC and a wireless network card and sign up for a data plan with your preferred cell phone provider. Instant Internet wherever you need it. Take a break at work and answer tickets. Or use that card in your laptop and bring it wherever you go. It's not a cheap solution, but if you have a Pocket PC or a laptop, it's not such a big expense anymore. You could also visit a Starbucks near work during lunch hours and sign up for the hot-spot Internet access.

Another option is to outsource work. Ask friends for help and pay them for their work. Very often friends are willing to help. If they do not want to be paid, pay them by taking them out to dinner or by providing free Web hosting and a domain name. You get the idea. If your wife or partner can do some work and has time and Internet access, get them to help you. Don't force friends or family to help you. It is not worth creating fights over this.

Make sure you have a cell phone with you at all times if you offer phone support. Again, if you are still employed with another company, don't misuse the time you are being paid for. Be fair to your boss and always remember, one day you will be the boss.

As mentioned before, many have been in this situation before you and many folks made it successfully through this transitional period. It is hard work and you might often be working 18 hour days. Never lose site of your goal. Stay focused.

The True Cost of Self-Employment

So you think you are now ready to make that jump and go from being an employee to full self-employment? The profit from your part-time business (so far) already matches your normal paycheck. You think it's now time to fire your boss and make a living without that paycheck from your employer.

Before you take that final step to personal freedom, make sure you really understand what you will be giving up. Do you know that your employer paid benefits that may cost you more than you realize if you have to pay for them yourself?

For most people, it will take much more than $50,000 of profit per year to replace a $50,000 annual salary. On average, an employer pays 25% to 35% on top of your salary for your benefits (this number may vary for businesses with less than 50 employees).

When we talk about what your employer pays for benefits, we're not referring to the "free" office supplies, subsidized or free soft drinks, coffee, or tea, or even the occasional free meal at the holiday party. The items that you need to think about are the benefits that are going to cost you the most money. We are talking about the employer's part of your health insurance premium, unemployment insurance, life insurance, 401K, and so on. So, to make up for all those things, your $50,000 salary suddenly needs to be around $65,000+ per year.

Based on a US Chamber of Commerce survey, medical insurance costs approximately 15% of an employee's salary. However, employers also cover the cost of many other forms of insurance which may include:

- Dental

- Vision

- Health

- Life

- Disability

- Unemployment

- Long Term Care Insurance

- Workers Compensation

You might be thinking that you pay premiums for these products already. Even if you do, your employer is most likely paying the larger share of the cost. Not to mention the fact that many times, the premiums you are paying are come out of your pre-tax dollars. This means you end up paying less in taxes because the amount of your premium is deducted prior to calculating your taxable income. Also keep in mind that the cost for health insurance has been going 10% a year or more for the past 4 years. This is a number that is most likely going to stay in the double-digits.

When you own your own business, not only are you responsible for the full cost of all forms of insurance paid out of after-tax dollars, you are going to be responsible for self-employment taxes, too. Self-employment taxes include the employer-paid portion of Social Security and Medicare taxes. This means your bill for these taxes will most likely double. Instead of paying 7.65% of your income for these, you will now be paying 15.30%.

And don't forget about having to pay estimated taxes. You will have to file and pay taxes quarterly now, instead of just once a year. Keep in mind that not properly paying taxes in advance will eventually come back as a boomerang in the form of late fees and penalties. Not only do your taxes increase, so do the headaches and the cost of filing! If you do not yet have an accountant, it is time to think about this more intensively.

If you have been receiving an employers match to your 401K, this money will now have to come out of your own pocket. You might not even be eligible for a 401K and will have to look into different forms of retirement accounts. A steep learning curves lies ahead.

These are only a few of items that normally make up 30 to 40% of your salary and will suddenly show up to haunt when you become self-employed. Then there are other things like discounted shopping at car dealerships, banks, or certain stores. If you have been depending on these perks, keep this in mind and budget those numbers accordingly.

I hope you don't think I am trying to discourage you from finally making the big step to self-employment. But this last step requires a little more planning than just walking into your boss's office and to slap down your letter of resignation. ;-)

Marketing
Advertising
Promotion

To be successful you will need to advertise your services to the public. The following sections will provide an in-depth look into very successful marketing and advertising steps (that is, if they are executed properly).

Advertising / Marketing Strategies

Advertising can be an art and if done wrong, the consequences for a start-up business can be disastrous. Here are a few things to keep in mind before trying to get the message out.

- Is your site search engine optimized?

- Have you tried marketing to your local market or are you just trying to use the Internet?

- Have you submitted any press releases?

- Do you have anyone linking to you?

- Do you have any banner advertising?

- Are you actively marketing your site/business DAILY?

- Are your prices to high or to low?

- What is your target group?

Local Advertising

Local advertising is often a much better and a much more affordable way to spread the word. Get your Web site listed in local business directories and in the Yellow Pages for your area. Check the advertising rates for local newspapers. Go to networking groups, Lead groups and/or to your local Chamber of Commerce and become a member. Get a sign for your car that shows your domain name and/or what kind of business you have. Bumper stickers are another good way to promote your business. Give them to friends and family to get your name out on the streets. Dress up a little bit, pack a stack of business cards, make a flyer, and visit small businesses in the strip malls in your area. Introduce yourself and try to make contact. Don't push things. Call them back a few days later and ask if they have any questions about your services. Go back a few days later and visit them again. You can buy mailing lists from the U.S. Postal service and even send out postcards to these lists. Business card-style advertisements in local newspapers are also a proven way to attract customers to your Web site or to get you a call from a customer who noticed the ad in the newspaper.

Here is one thing to keep in mind; the biggest mistake businesses do in advertising, is contacting a customer only once. Be persistent and follow up on sales leads whenever you can. 60% to 70% of what you spend on advertising is most likely a complete waste of money.

Cheap Advertising

Is it possible to advertise for almost no cost? Yes, it is. Word of mouth can be very effective for promoting your business. Give away a few free accounts to friends, their friends, and to your relatives. Make sure they all experience the best service possible and motivate them to tell everyone about it. Become a contributing member in online forums. Don't SPAM the forums. Deliver content and take advantage of the signature area at the bottom of each of your postings to discreetly announce what you are doing. Yes, you could visit Web hosting forums like WHT, but in most cases you will meet your competition, not customers. Visit forums for other interests. Do you have any hobbies? Search for forums related to your hobby and become a contributor there. If your postings and contributions are of good nature and provide solid information, you will get sales inquiries from other forum members, sooner or later. Be persistent. Be pro-active and be prepared.

SPAM Advertising

Should you use SPAM to advertise your services? No. The local SPAM laws are getting tougher every year anyway. Also, most people are annoyed by SPAM e-mail. A business that uses SPAM advertising might see a short spike in sales inquiries, but in the long run, it will destroy any reputation it might have. Stay away from SPAM.

Advertising with Google Adwords

How about Google Adwords? Does it make sense for a startup business to use it for advertising? Using Google Adwords for advertising a Web hosting business can be very expensive. If you are on a budget, there are certainly better ways to spend advertising money for your business. If you are willing to spend a significant amount of money and your target group is not local businesses, give it a try. It can be very effective, if done right.

Business Cards

It's always good to have at least two different sets of business cards. If you need to impress, hand out the one that says you are the owner, CEO or president. If you talk to a client and do not want to make the impression that you are a one-person shop and do it all yourself, hand out the business card that says you're the Technical Director - Web Hosting or that you are a "Hosting Specialist". You get the idea. As long as you do not lie to the customer, you will be fine.

Define Your Target Group

Don't even think about considering "everyone" as your target group. It won't work and you will be disappointed by the results if you try. In marketing, there are two approaches: the "shotgun" approach and the "rifle" approach. I am not sure how familiar with guns you are. For the sake of explanation, I will assume not very.

A shotgun fires many little balls or bullets that spray in a fan pattern. When you fire it, you can only aim in a general direction and hope to hit the target.

A rifle shoots a single projectile at a clearly defined target. You need to focus on this target (market).

Rifle marketing or niche marketing is the best method for a company when it is a small business.

Shotgun marketing is similar to what big companies do, like Coca Cola or McDonalds. They have the money to skim people off the top; you don't. Find a small group to target, specialize in the group, focus on them. Eat, sleep, and breathe ideas about how you can better serve that group. You have to have a clearly set goal; do not stray from that goal. (Note: I would like to thank Derrick for providing part of this article and the permission to use it here.)

Negative Advertising? Don't!

Ever considered negative advertising?

Attacking a competitor is never a good way of advertising. Don't point out the faults of others. It will come back one day and haunt you. The selfishness of a negative marketing campaign is apparent and will put many consumers off of even looking at your products and services. It looks unfair and cheap, unprofessional. This form of advertising simply creates a feeling of mistrust. But if others do it, why shouldn't you?

Studies have shown that many people actually think that the company who runs negative ads does not have anything positive to show about itself. It creates the feeling that you are not proud of your products and you would rather hide behind the possible weaknesses of your competitor. Your audience wants to see positive things. Life is already tough and dirty enough. By pointing out the negative, you are not providing what everyone is looking for.

Do you have any idea why movies that portray the perfect lives of perfect people in a perfect environment are so successful? These movies show what everyone is dreaming about. Most people know that it is just a movie but deep down inside, everyone is dreaming of this perfect world. It creates positive feelings toward the movie. The same principles are true for advertising. Show the bright side of life, the happy and attractive side. Have people associate your products with these positive feelings, not with the dark and uninviting side of life.

Are you are old enough to remember the Coca Cola TV spots of the 1980's and early 1990's? Beautiful and successful people, great music, tons of fun, and right in the middle of it all, the product (Coke). It created the clear association that Coke was part of the fun and that beautiful and successful people only drink Coke. This is the effect you are targeting in your advertising. If you do the opposite, you create negative associations with your product, even if your product is superior and outperforms your competitor three to one. Compare the results of two ads, one negative, one positive. One going the negative route, one the positive route. One trashing your competitor, the other praising the strength and quality of your own products. You will be surprised. You will find that the positive ad out pulls in front of the other four to one.

Think positive. Let your ads show it.

Using Flyers for Marketing

A very inexpensive way to promote your business is to create different kind of flyers and distribute them wherever you go. Pin your flyers to bulletin boards at the supermarket, the library, bookstore. Hand them out at networking events, or at tennis practice.

Here are a few easy tips on how to make your flyers noticeable:

1). **Include your picture on the flyer**:
   People connect better with others visually. Color is great, but black and white will work, too.

2). **Snappy headline:**
   Hook your prospective customers with the headline in the top line. For example, Read About Web Hosting as It Really Is! Give them a real reason to read your flyer and not to toss it away. Demonstrate those benefits!

3). **Call to action:**
   The flyer needs to promote a call for action. What do you want the reader to do once they read the flyer? Call you? Visit your Web site? A common mistake is not to include a call for action.

4). **Spell out the steps:**
   When selling your product, make it easy for the reader to purchase your product. Show them how they can order online, via fax, or by phone (works best in local markets). Here is a great example of some possible wording: "3 Easy Steps for Ordering." Make sure you tell them when they can expect to receive the account information. For skeptics, offer them a URL link to your Web site to get more information.

5). Identify yourself:

Let the flyer tell your potential customers that you are a local guy and not some anonymous company from XYZ. Small Mom and Pop businesses especially like to work with local guys.

6). Get the working right:

The headline must grab the reader's attention. The first paragraph must hold them. You only have, on average, three seconds to accomplish this. If you are looking for a specific target market, find out what words/phrases will get their attention and develop your wording specifically for that audience. Experiment with several versions to see what works and what does not until you get the response you want.

7). Take them with you:

Carry at least 20-30 flyers with you in a sealed plastic folder. This protects them from the elements and looks professional when you take one out to give to the person you are talking to.

8). Make the flyers worth more:

When talking to people, use the back-side of the flyer to write down notes. People tend to hold on to them longer that way. You can write a special code for a special discount on the backside. Make sure it will "expire" some time soon. This will force the reader into action if he or she wants to take advantage of the offer. Tell them what the code means and ask that they provide it when they e-mail or call. Design the codes so that they mean something to you. It makes it easier for you to remember who you gave it to.

Stand Out From the Competition

Attract new clients by offering a benefit that is different from those of everyone else. What is your distinct advantage? What separates you from the competition?

Visiting your competitors' Web sites will give you ideas about content, design, and features you may need for your own Web site in order to become more successful and to attract more visitors. Then, update your Web site and also design marketing materials that stand out and distinguish you from the competition.

- Answer the following questions to yourself to help you to find your niche.

- Why should customers buy Web hosting from you instead of your competitors?

- Do you offer a free consultation, initial visit, analysis, Web site migration services, or better customer service?

- What are the most important benefits or results your customers will achieve by using your Web hosting services?

- What can you do better than anyone else? Do you possess hard-to-find or specialized expertise?

- What makes your products and services more outstanding, unique, and more desirable than your competitors?

- Do you keep customers informed with newsletters, service update notifications or even an information hotline?

- Do you have the lowest prices or the highest quality products in the hosting industry?

- Do you provide the fastest service, the strongest guarantee, longest hours, the best SLA, or the best follow up?

You will need to determine what makes your business unique. Then you can emphasize your uniqueness to make your Web site and marketing materials stand out from the crowd and set you apart from your competition.

Business Cards

Business cards can be an important marketing tool, if created and used properly. Put them to use wherever you can. A business card can be a very effective marketing tool when doing offline marketing. But there some "dos" and "don'ts" to keep in mind when using business cards to promote your business.

Design
White business cards with only black printing are completely out. They are boring and don't really turn anyone on. When you design your business cards, make sure that there is something about it that will make the person you gave it to want to look at the card. Exciting scenery or landscapes or something related to your business or industry are options for the background of your business card. You could also have your own photo printed on your business card. It will be different from what most people have seen in the past and will therefore stick in their minds, meaning that they will remember you and your business. You will only get the message across if you can get people to look at your card.

Content
Do not overload the business card with information. The business card needs to have your basic business information and a hint of what your business has to offer. If you are a Web host, have your business name printed on the card plus "Web Hosting" or "Web Hosting Provider".

Message or Slogan
The business card should also have your company slogan or marketing message printed on it, if you have one. If you have a good one line slogan or marketing message that is catchy and worth remembering, put it on your business card.

Logo
The same is true for your logo. If your business logo catches the eye, put it on your business card.

If you don't have an eye-catching logo or you don't have one at all, use something else that catches your customer's attention. A great, exciting looking background on a business card is an effective way to make the person you give it to notice.

Put Added Value on Your Business Card

This will cause people to keep it in their wallet or somewhere else where they will handle it often. If your town or city has a well-liked sports team, get the game schedule printed on the back-side of your business card. Fans will keep it handy and this means your business name will be around and visible. Another option is to print a coupon on the backside of your business card. People who are interested in your services or products will keep it around until they decide to use the coupon. Make sure the coupon is not time-limited Just imagine having a stack of 500 business cards with an expired coupon printed on the backside.

When to Use Your Card

When should you use your business card? Give it to customers whenever you can. If you send out letters, invoices or estimates, attach your business card to the letter. Give it out at church, seminars, meetings. Post it on bulletin boards at supermarkets or community-related places. Leave two or three in the locker room at the gym every time you go there.

Keep them handy so that you can give it out at any time. Keep a stack of business cards in your car or truck, your briefcase, your wallet, in your planner, at home, anywhere you can think of where you might have a chance to hand it to somebody.

Another good thing you can do with your business card is to not only carry it around with you, but have other people (friends, family) carry it and pass it around for you. If you have employees, don't be cheap. Get business cards for them, too. In most cases, having a business card raises the self-esteem of your employees (it makes them feel valuable and accepted) and they will use it. This will get your business name out to even more people.

If you attend seminars or tradeshows, make sure to drop your card in the "fish bowls" or card collection boxes. The same is true for restaurants who offer free lunches for one of their customers drawn from the pool of business cards dropped into a bowl. When you put your card in the bowl, manually place it on the outside where it might be visible to other folks.

The Importance of Quality

If you print them yourself, make sure they look professional. If they create the impression that they are home-made and cheap, don't do it. Having them printed at a professional print shop will give you the piece of mind that they will look good and professional. In most cases, it will be cheaper, too. Make sure the quality is excellent, no matter if you print them yourself or have them printed. A non-durable business card will make a bad impression. Make sure your business card is legible. If it is too difficult to read because of a small font size, nobody will really read it.

Appropriate Placing

The old myth of placing "some on the table when you leave a restaurant" is a waste of your resources. First of all in every restaurant, the tables will be cleaned before the next guest will be seated. The person who usually cleans the table is probably not your target group at all. This is a low wage job and these poor souls have different concerns. Rather check with the restaurant manager to see if you can leave a couple near the cash register.

Seven Creative Ways to Do Marketing

There are plenty of ways to let customers know about your products. Why not use things that are already in place for communication with clients?

Invoices

Fill your invoice statements with special offers or information about new products and services. Either add small brochures or flyers to the invoice letter or print your marketing message on the invoice itself. Remember, you are already paying for postage. So why not fully utilize this part of the business?!

Cash Register Receipts

If you generate receipts for your customers, they should include more than just a transaction record. If your cash register allows it, print a small marketing message at the bottom of each receipt. Or have it print out a second receipt that you can also hand the customer. Target, for example, always prints out two receipts for the client. The first one is a regular receipt. The second one is in case the customer has bought a present and does not want to hand the real receipt to the person receiving the present but still allowing the item to be returned. It actually reminds the customer about buying presents at Target. You could use the same method of making customers aware of your current specials.

Occasion Cards

Send birthday cards, Thanksgiving cards, congratulations cards. They are a great way to let customers know you care. This builds a very high level of customer loyalty.

Partner Up

By partnering with other businesses in your marketing efforts, you can dramatically expand your results. Here is an example: A Web hosting business teams up with a local ISP (Internet Service Provider) or with a local Web designer. The Web designer uses your services for Web hosting, while you refer any client to him who needs a Web site built.

Run a Contest

People love contests. Just look at the huge success of game shows on television. People even love to see other people win! Why don't you run your own contest? If you choose to develop a promotional contest, make sure it is not a plain boring contest. Make it fun, make it silly, and don't forget to really hype it up. If your contest is wacky and crazy enough, you might be able to even get some good media coverage (mainly local radio stations or perhaps local newspapers). This is free advertising for your business.

Giveaways

You are probably wondering how you can make money if you are giving away your products free of charge?! Well, it's a lot easier and less expensive than paying for a real advertising campaign. In fact, giveaways have their place in just about any type of business.

For consumer retail businesses, you may want to offer your product for free trial periods, or offer free estimates if you are in a service-oriented business. Let's assume you are selling computer peripherals. Give away that nice, cool looking printer for free, and make the money on selling paper and extra ink cartridges. Once a customer is in your store, he might buy something.

Limit the giveaways to the first 10 customers per hour or for a given time period during the day. Many people will come, not everyone gets something for free, but maybe some will buy something from you anyway.

Giveaways work very well on the Internet, too. If you have a nice online store, spread the word through Web sites like Fatwallet.com or Techbargains.com (and many others).

Packaging is King

"Don't judge a book by its cover," the old saying states, but as a book publisher, I can tell you that the cover is exactly how most people judge books. If you walk around in a retail store, it is the odd-looking packages that stand out and grab the attention of the shopper. Use the same principle for your products, no matter if it is online or offline retailing.

The End Defines the Beginning

Timing Your Pitch

Potential clients will remember best what you say last. When doing your sales pitch, make a big 'finale' out of it. So in one sense, the end of your sales presentation will be the beginning for your clients. Did you know that speakers often reach their momentum in the middle of the presentation and then lose contact with the audience by the end of the show?! One way a speaker (YOU) can ensure a new beginning for the audience (your future clients) is by having a very strong ending.

Focus on Your Purpose

First, focus on the general purpose of your sales presentation. Are you moving the audience to action at all? Does your audience understand how you and your services will help them generate a better return of investment (ROI)? Or are you simply being entertaining (wasting their time, in this case)? The purpose of your sales speech is to get the clients to want your services badly enough for you to be able to close a deal. Some speakers lose sight of this. Their endings do not fit their purposes, and the audience will wonder what the actual purpose of the speech and the visit really was about.

Make Them Want You

The purpose of your speech it to get the clients wanting your services, and wanting them now. Prepare your speech accordingly. You will most likely be talking to business owners. Show them how hosting a Web site with you will increase their ability to sell their own products. At the end, the clients need to know if they don't start any action they are already losing out. They have to come to the conclusion that they need to get started right away.

That Catchy Phrase

It is very important for you to summarize all the benefits of your services. Create a catchy phrase that will stay in their mind for a while. Make them think about it, make them remember you. A solid exit phrase is the key for a new beginning. The exit line will increase the likelihood of the audience remembering what you want them to do after the presentation as they make their new beginning.

Be Prepared

I can't stress it enough. Be prepared. A former senator (Bill Bradley) once said, "When you are not practicing, remember, someone somewhere is practicing…and when you meet him, he will win." Practicing means preparing for this situation. It might make sense to buy a book with the quotes of great people. Something they said that is worth being printed in a book might be something worth using in your sales presentation. Make sure you let your audience know who originally said that quote.

Concluding

A good way to enhance the ending of your speech is to understand the mechanics of a conclusion. It should be short. Don't start concluding when you still have ten minutes of material left to talk about. Don't say, "In conclusion…" unless you really intend on finishing. You will lose the attention of your audience if you continue talking long after you announce you are finishing.

Speak the conclusion without reading it. Look at your audience as you end; know exactly what you want to say and avoid fumbling with your notes. This will distract people from the importance of your words. The ending should raise the emotional level of your interaction with the audience. Look pleasant and try not to hide as you end. Be present, be visible. Conclusions are great opportunities to move away from the lectern and toward the audience. Do not introduce new stuff when making a conclusion.

This will distract people from the message you were selling before.

Finally, don't take the ending too seriously. Don't expect a standing ovation. Let the ending sink in. Prepare a follow up soon. Do not wait too long to close the deal. Concentrate on the ending in order to create a new beginning (that is, a new customer).

More Marketing Strategies

In marketing your business, it's easy to find a way that produces many leads or potential clients, but is it wise to only use that one avenue? It is important to diversify and find several outlets in which to market your business, your products, and services, both online and offline. Achieving a good balance is the key.

Create Synergy

Find others that serve the same audience but are not your competitors. Hook up with them and promote each other. Two are always better than one! In the case of Web hosting, this could be local Web designers or even computer repair shops.

Today's society is bombarded with advertising and marketing messages. E-mail (SPAM), telemarketing, regular mail, solicitation at your front door. How can you make your marketing and advertising stand out in of this flood of marketing messages and be effective in your target market?

Listen to Your Customers

Take the time to listen and relate to the problems of your clients. Keep in mind that it is much easier to sell a good solution to a problem than to only sell positive benefits or specific features.

What problems are your potential clients really facing? What can you offer to make those problems go away?

A great way to find out is to spend more time networking and doing market research by contacting potential clients. Find out what their real needs are by spending time asking questions and listening to their answers, taking mental note of their needs, problems, and problem areas. If one or two clients have certain problem areas, you can safely assume that there are more clients with similar problems.

Study the Problem

Once you see a (recurring) problem that your product or service can solve, study that problem, and adjust your marketing so that it is offering THE benefit and THE solution to that problem. If you properly identify a problem and make the necessary adjustments, success will be yours. When drafting your new marketing plan, be sure to describe the problem and the solution. This will keep your marketing efforts from heading into the wrong direction.

Evaluate

After implementing a new marketing program, entrepreneurs must evaluate its performance or they risk wasting money. Every program should have performance standards to compare with the actual results. Researching industry norms and past performance will help you develop appropriate standards, and therefore, help you find out if your new marketing campaign is really successful.

Create an Effective Strategy

It is very difficult to get your potential customers to notice your ads, let alone even respond to them. Because advertising is so expensive, you should use a clear strategy in order to concentrate your advertising impact in the most effective manner. The only exception to this advertising rule might be for advertising in the Yellow Pages or other yearly publications (for example, business directories).

Especially when starting out it, is critical to reach the masses and to gain a solid customer base. In a situation like this, one strategy could be spending a big chunk of your advertising funds on one big campaign. A concentrated campaign on some very busy Web sites can do the trick. Imagine advertising on Sitepoint and WebHostingTalk at the same time for one week. Use a highly visible spot and your sign-up Web page could become very busy.

Quarterly advertising campaigns are quite common and are a very good tool. They will allow you to concentrate your advertising dollars heavily during specific times, while also affording you a better chance of maintaining a place in the minds of your targeted audience throughout the whole year.

Many small businesses completely spend away their advertising money throughout the year by placing a continuous stream of small ads all over the place. This kind of approach never creates enough impact to deliver significant results. Which of the following do you think will be noticed better: a large advertisement placed in a highly visible spot for one week per month or per quarter or a small ad hidden at the bottom of a newspaper page every day? If you are using the small ad system, stop it - now. Drop all advertising for a while and see if the number of new sign-ups really falls off. It probably won't, and you can then feel confident in adopting a new advertising schedule.

Elements of a Successful Advertising Campaign

A successful marketing campaign needs certain elements to be successful. The following information will help you develop a successful marketing campaign.

Establish a Feeling of Urgency in the Buyer

Basically, tell your customers, "you need to sign up today because it will help you reach your goals." Don't tell your customer the offer will still be as good tomorrow as it is today; they must buy today! Urgency! Study how successful ads make the customer act now. Remember the X10 Spy Cam advertising campaign? They always had their Web site set up with a deadline for a special deal. Something like that is easy to program and will eventually urge the customer to sign up today. Don't over do it. Use this tactic for a week, then switch to something else. Rotate these marketing tools. Start looking more closely at the marketing vehicles (e-mail, letters, postcards,) you receive yourself every day, and you'll begin to see that effective marketing always gives you a reason to act now.

Show the Benefits

Show a list of benefits if the customer signs up with you. There must be a list of benefits to make him sign up. Will you be smarter using your services? Will he get more visitors? Will your server be better than the competitions hardware? Will your business help to make the site more successful? Or make him richer, or healthier, or faster? Focus on the client, not the advertiser. Most benefits need to be skillfully integrated into the ad. It is a waste of time and money in an ad or on your Web site if you don't work in the benefits and present them properly.

Call to Action

Tell them what they must do to get what you are offering. Don't assume that your prospects and customers will figure out how to get it. They won't do your work for you. So, go ahead and tell them what to do. If they have to call you to get it, then tell them to call (to call you now!). If they have to write or drop a post card in the mail, or fax something to you, then tell them clearly and in words easy to understand. The point is to make it as easy as possible for your target customer to do what you want them to do. People don't like to do anything that is going to take work on their part. Make it as easy for them to respond as possible, or they won't, which, of course, is not the result you want.

Do It Again

You must tell customers what to do, that is, to sign up with you. Tell your customer to order now - this very moment. So many ads assume that the customer will guess how to fill out the contact form, e-mail you, or telephone for the information, or product. Tell the customer what to do. Provide the customer exact instructions on how to respond today in several ways. The more options you can offer, the better the results will be.

Schedule Effectively

Plan your advertising calendar and campaign several months in advance. Failure to plan advertising in advance will waste a lot of your money. Rush charges, poor design, rate increases, poor creative input and poor copy are common results of failing to plan in advance. "I didn't have enough time," "I was under the gun to get this placed," are common phrases heard under rushed circumstances. Take a blank calendar and fill in the days, months, or quarters when it is best to advertise in your target markets. Figure out the number of sensible ad insertions and negotiate a contract with various media suppliers (for example, in local newspapers). Book banner space well in advance on important Web sites. Prepare your Web site with a special landing page for the expected visitors.

Test your banners and your ads

Only by trial and error will you be able to set a baseline as to the best response rates for your ads and banners. It is very important to maximize response in relation to the number of dollars spent. Sometimes re-phrasing text or adjusting the ad layout can make the difference between a low or average response and a great success and high ROI (Return on Investment). You will need to find out what works best for your business. After you find this out, you'll want to stay on course and base future advertising campaigns on the success of the old one.

Be Honest

Avoid misleading or dishonest advertising in hopes of duping readers/Web site visitors into using your products or services. Honesty and integrity are the primary key to repeat sales and repeat business. If you have to trick your audience to get their attention, you will have a very hard time keeping their attention and their business if they sign up at all.

Run Events on Your Site

Running events on your Web site is an excellent way to encourage repeat traffic and repeat visitors. You'll want to begin running events once traffic from your site launch begins to fade. Examples include contests, games, on-line interviews, chat sessions and maybe even audio broadcasts. Do the things your competitors don't do.

Marketing and Advertising Back-to-Back Basics

The following information may apply to your situation, or not. There is no one way to do it right in every case. Grab the ideas here and play with them. Marketing has to be dynamic. A successful strategy in one market does not guarantee success in a different market.

Always Follow Up

Why do businesses lose customers? Poor service? Poor quality? High prices? In most cases a business loses customers because they do not follow up. It's like apathy after the sale. The business basically ignores the customers.

Did you know that the cost of selling something to a new customer is about six times higher than selling something to an existing customer? So, what can you do about this?

Follow up on every sale and on every sales inquiry. If a customer buys your products and you have his e-mail address, send a thank you note within 48 hours after the sale. Send another note about 30 days after the initial sale and ask how things are going and if the customer has any concerns or problems. Make sure the customer knows that you care. Even if there might be a problem, knowing that you care will give the customer that warm, fuzzy feeling that he needs to feel comfortable using your service. Make it a habit of following up every quarter thereafter.

Inform customers about new products, features and services. Let them know what you did to make their stay more worth while and that they have the option of upgrading their hosting package whenever they need to. The next quarter, offer referral fees to motivate the client to recommend your services to friends and family. Once the first year anniversary arrives, offer the customer a freebie or a discount for a domain name renewal or registration. Offer a 10% discount on the next higher hosting package. You get the idea. Stay in touch with the client and build a friendly relationship. This will make it harder for the customer to leave or to yell at you when something goes wrong with your service. Friends don't yell at friends, right!?

Keep Your Best Customers Happy

Not all customers are created 'equal'. Some spend more money on your service, always pay on time, and are simply pleasant to deal with. Support tickets are random and they don't create much work for you. They don't complain about a reasonable price adjustment. Those are your "A1" customers. Treat them like family. If you treat them right and (again) give them the warm, fuzzy feeling they need to feel comfortable, they will refer your services to friends and family.

As mentioned before, not all customers are equal. I am very sure that you put your customers into certain groups. The range probably goes from customers that you hate to the customers you love. Treat the ones that are most beneficial to your business with the best service possible. It'll pay off in the long run.

Create an Elevator Speech

In today's world, it is important for every business owner to compose an elevator speech for himself. If you think an elevator speech is only to be used in elevators, you're wrong. The term "elevator speech" represents the time span you have to introduce your business to someone else. If you do not have a quick way to describe your business and your services and the value you give to your customers, you might lose out on many sales occasions. Imagine waiting in line at the bank or at the supermarket. You make typical small talk. Guess what? If you have an elevator speech prepared, you can use the moment to promote your business. Think about it. There are probably tons of situations where you could use your elevator speech to promote your business.

The elements of a good elevator speech are easy to recognize. Your elevator speech should describe the value you have to offer and what the benefits are to your customers. It should encourage the listener to speak and to ask you about your business. The elevator speech should last less than 30 seconds. Learn your lines by heart and make it sound confident and impressive.

Press Releases

Make use of free media reports. Publish a press release whenever possible. The occasion has to be noteworthy, of course. Newspapers, magazines, radio and TV, they all receive press releases from the newswires. A local newspaper might catch on and will contact you to write a story about you and your business. Look into the business section of your local newspaper. How often do you see a report about a local business? Where I live, it happens quite often. Maybe the newspaper publishes company profiles every once in a while. Maybe you'll the chosen one.

How does one publish a press release? You should find out how to directly submit a press release to your local newspaper. It might require some work, but newspapers are always looking for information that they can publish. Use services like PRWeb.com to publish your press release. PRWeb.com even offers templates so that you know what a professional press release looks like.

Communicate Your Personality

Every business has a company personality. Many customers stay loyal to a business because of its personality. If your business looks just like everyone else's, people will not really remember you. You will lose sales. If there is something that will stick to people's minds, they will remember you.

To use 'personality' as part of your marketing strategy, you will have to develop a personality. What is personality? There are two key words that you will need to remember: image and identity. You could try to establish an image or you could try to establish an identity. You probably always thought that you will need to have a good image in your industry. You build up an image, something that you think people will respond to. Guess what? People will feel that it is just an image. They will feel that this is not the real you. They will feel that you and/or your employees are not 100% connected to your business. Sooner or later people will realize that it is just an image, not the real thing.

Identity

Identity expresses your personality as it really is. Your identity does not lie or sound phony. The identity is exactly how the business has portrayed itself. People will feel this and it creates trust. Trust is the seed to getting business from the customer. And the best thing is, there is no cost involved in communicating your identity (personality). You are who you are. Just live up to it.

The Number 9

Did you know that, on average, a customer to sees your business name or advertisement nine times before they purchase your services and/or products?! Did you know that you have to try three time before a customer consciously sees your business name or advertisement at all? Do the math. This means that you have to try 27 times before the customer buys your service or product. Did you know that most business don't realize that it takes, on average, 27 tries to win the customer and that they stop their specific marketing efforts basically half-way through. The moment those businesses stop is actually the moment when the customer starts realizing that he is maybe even interested in their services or products. He is not convinced yet, but he will remember your business name. What a waste of marketing dollars this is. What does this mean for you? You will need patience. You will need thorough planning when creating a marketing campaign. You will need to be persistent. Get your message out but do not give up right away. Remember, the potential customer has to consciously see your ad about nine times before buying your services.

Turning Customer Complaints into Sales

Complaints offer companies amazing insight and the chance to improve their services. However, many companies do not value them as much as they really should, and many try to avoid receiving them at all. Complaints shed light on where your company might be falling short and where you could excel. Negative feedback can be used as a driving force behind product and service enhancement, new offerings, and outbound sales and marketing campaigns. Analyze each situation carefully.

$%!? Happens

You can never eliminate customer complaints. If you are running a business, no matter what the size, customers will complain at some point. Mistakes will happen regardless of how carefully you try to prevent them. Expect to get a few complaints periodically. It's part of operating a business. But you can and should plan for complaints. Proper planning will help you make the best out of customer complaints. Always handle customer complaints with a positive attitude. Smile while talking to the customer on the phone or when you write an e-mail message. It does not matter if you are responsible for what happened or if the customer made a mistake and is blaming it on you. Make your customers happy now and they will reward you with more sales later on.

Surprise Your Customer

Surprise your customer with a fast response to his or her complaint. If you can't solve the problem right away, make sure that you keep a good level of communication alive. Nothing bothers people more than feeling ignored, especially in touchy situations like this. The longer a customer has to worry about getting the problem solved, the less likely he will accept a solution and remain your customer.

Grade the Complaint

Grade the level of the complaint. If you did screw up, fix it. Don't make the customer responsible for your mistakes. Let the customer know that you made a mistake and what your plan is. Let him know what you learned from the situation and what you will do to prevent future situations from happening. If it is the customers fault, decide if it is worth keeping this customer. If the customer has never been a problem and does not seem to be a troublemaker, it is well worth keeping him and making him happy, if the price is reasonable. Don't just look only at the short-term, but also consider the mid to long term.

Take Responsibility

You have decided to solve the issue and to take the blame. Congratulations. Take responsibility for resolving your customer's complaint even if the problem was not your fault. Apologize for the inconvenience to the customer. Briefly summarize the situation and explain the cause of the problem. Don't lie. But good wording can help you here. Explaining your mistake properly presents you as a person who knows what happened and is still in control. Don't blame someone else for the problem. It sounds like a cheap excuse.

Get Referrals

Now it is time to make the winning move and turn this customer into a person who creates referrals for your business. Surprise the customer by solving the problem AND by giving him something extra to compensate for the inconvenience. This will put the customer in the position of having receiving something for free. He feels honored and obligated. He will feel he came out of the situation with the upper hand. This helps the customer to a) forget about the initial problem, and b) remember the special attention you gave him when others ask about your services.

Follow Up

Follow up on the customer after a few days and again after a month. Make sure that the customer is happy. Of course, if you caused the problem, make sure that it won't happen again. You might not have a second chance and the market out there is brutal. Your competitors are just waiting for you to make mistakes.

Document

While others just move on after getting a complaint out of the way, you should take the·time to write everything down. It could be some sort of a journal or a professional complaint database software that you have purchased. Keep track of every complaint and come back frequently to revisit each item. Make sure that you are not falling short in avoiding similar situations. Handling a touchy situation properly can result in increased sales and higher customer satisfaction.

Corporate Holiday Gifts - Good for Marketing?

It's that time of the year again. The first Christmas greeting cards are arriving in the mail. Customers or businesses you do work with send you holiday greetings. Some even send you presents. Now you feel obligated. This is often the reason why someone sends you presents or holiday greetings to your business.

Do you use corporate holiday gifts to keep your customers happy and to grow your business? Or are you just sitting tight and not doing anything at all? Maybe it is time to work out a marketing strategy that includes corporate holiday gifts or at least holiday greetings to your most important customers. So what are your options?

E-Mail Blast

Send a friendly Christmas greeting (or to be political correct, a holiday greeting) via e-mail to all your customers. Thank them for their patronage and wish them the best for the holidays and for the next year.

Snail-Mail Holiday Postcards

Everyone loves to get snail mail. Especially if it is not a bill or an invoice. Sending out Christmas Cards via snail mail is a nice way to thank you customers. You're probably limited to local or domestic customers since international postage would increase your postage costs too much.

Corporate Holiday Presents

Perhaps consider sending small Christmas presents to your most important customers. A nice pen engraved with your company logo, a stress-relieving ball, or other small signs of your appreciation work well. Do you have that one big customer that brings you a lot of business? Maybe it would be worth it to step up a little bit. A friend of mine once received a box of fresh Salmon delivered from of Alaska to his front door in Europe.

Now that is something he still remembers. Maybe do something similar. How about Omaha Steaks? Or a DVD player?

Take Notes

Start taking notes through-out the year if you meet with clients or talk to them via e-mail, IM, or over the phone. If they mention things they like or dislike, it might give you a good hint of what to buy or not to buy for them. By early November, you should have a good impression of how to surprise those really important customers. Plan for this early enough to avoid problems and stress when the Christmas season arrives.

Yes, of course, these efforts will cost you a bit of money, but the marketing effect can be quite long-lasting. And a good relationship with your customers will ensure that your business will continue to thrive, and that based on an existing customer base.

Google Adwords Guide

You probably have already heard about the new marketing tool from Google.com on the Internet. Their advertising service is called "Adwords" and allows you to use Google.com for marketing. When people initiate a search, your ads are displayed on Google's Web site. Your ads can also be prominently displayed on many thousands of targeted Web sites that are partners with Google in a program called "Google AdSense". Adwords is the Google.com version of the pay-per-click advertising model. That means users click on your ad and are redirected to your Web site or a specific URL that you have indicated while creating your ad campaign.

What do you need to know about Adwords? Adwords is a way to spend a lot of money on advertising very very quickly. BUT, Adwords is also a way to spend marketing money on a very selective or targeted audience. Adwords can be very expensive for the advertiser if not properly planned and tested.

When you setup a Google Adwords ad campaign, you choose certain keywords that will cause your ad to appear on a Google.com search results page. You also specify the maximum amount of money that you are willing to pay for each click. Remember, the **Google Adwords** program is a PPC (pay-per-click) model, so you only pay when someone actually clicks on your ad and then visits your Web site.

Keywords

It is very important to select the right keywords for your business ad. Keywords that are too generic and that everyone enters will not only be very ineffective but also very expensive. Play a little bit with the Adwords keyword and campaign settings just to get a feeling of how expensive the generic keywords for your business and industry are. You will soon realize that you need to be creative and careful with choosing keywords.

Google recommends using different spelling variations and plural versions of your keywords to reach the best target audience. This is a good approach since not every one uses keywords the same way when doing a search. Some people will use plural versions and others will use singular versions.

Exact matching of keywords in Google user queries requires you to place square brackets around your selected keywords, for example, [Web hosting]. Your ad will now only show when users enter the exact phrase 'Web hosting'. Your ad will not show if other words are included in the search string or the words are entered in a different order.

Phrase Option

Another keyword matching option is the phrase option. This is very similar to the exact matching of keywords in a search in the sense that the keywords must all be present and in the right order. However your ad will still show up in search results even if other words are present in the search. To make use of phrase matching, you must include your keywords in quotes, for example, "Web hosting".

Negative Matching

Negative matching is the final option available for your Adwords advertisement. This option allows you to prevent your ad from being shown if a certain word is present in the search query. This allows you to reduce the number of possible clicks on your ad in non-relevant searches and, therefore, to keep your costs lower. It also helps you make sure that your ad is not shown to users who will not be interested in your products. If your keyword is 'Web hosting' but your Web hosting is based on a Linux operating system and not on a Windows operating system, you can use negative matching to make sure your ad is not shown in search queries which include 'windows Web hosting'. In this case 'windows' would be your negative keyword. You simply place a dash in front of your negative keyword to use this option, for example, -windows.

Using the different ways of selecting keywords described here will help you be more successful with Google Adwords. Google also lets you be very specific as in which geographical area your ads will be displayed. The settings go from global to country, right down to specific states or cities. It is now much easier, especially for local businesses, to use Google Adwords for specific local markets.

Test Them Out

Well, you got the idea how to be very specific how you select your keywords and combinations of keywords. But how do you actually select the right keywords? In order to get the most out of Adwords, you must have a list of great keyword and phrases. If your keyword list is not good enough, you will suffer the consequences by paying too much for advertising. Write down all the top search terms that you can think of. Ask friends and family how they would use Google to find your product (without searching for the business name itself).

A competitor of Google actually offers a free tool that allows you to find out how popular your keywords are. Download this free tool here and use it to your advantage:

http://inventory.overture.com/d/searchinventory/suggestion/

Create a list of the most popular keywords. Now add more words to the popular keywords. Use words that describe your specific product or service. Now use these phrases or word combinations when setting up a Google Adwords campaign to find out how much you would have to pay per click to get your ad onto the first page in a Google search.

If the keywords you selected are very expensive to use, you should consider rewording or using different combinations. Maybe concentrate on a certain niche to find lower-priced keyword options.

How Often and When

When testing new campaigns, make sure that you limit your exposure by the amount of money you want to spend per day as well as by how long the campaign should last. It's easier to activate a campaign again if it is successful. If you fail to set limits, you might wind up spending lots of money in a very short time. This is money you can't get back.

Another way to save money on your Adwords advertising campaign is to wait for the end of the month. It's funny, but many folks follow a certain rule that says they should start their advertising at the beginning of the month. By the time the 25th of the month arrives, they have spent most of their money on their campaigns already. For you, this means that the prices for many popular keywords might be more affordable for you.

If your ads are advertising specific products, link to the specific product page and not to your homepage. 95% of the people who click through to your Web site will not be willing to start another search on your Web site to find the product mentioned in your ad.

Conclusion

Frequently revisit your campaigns and compare prices and results. The Internet is a rapidly changing environment. What works one day, might not necessarily work the next day. Keep track of everything, perhaps in a spreadsheet.

Writing and Publishing Articles as a Marketing Tool

During my own research on how to make my Web site "www.Webhostingresourcekit.com" more successful, I discovered that publishing a few of my articles on other Web sites created quite a bit of feedback in the form of additional traffic. I spent a lot of time analyzing my server log files to see where referrals would come from. To my own surprise,. I discovered that two articles submitted to other Web sites had gotten me good traffic and live return links to my Web site (usually a requirement if someone publishes your articles on your Web site).

So by publishing some of my articles on other Web sites, I am getting additional visitors to my Web site and a return link which helps increase the search engine ranking of my Web site. Publishing articles this way does not get you any cash, but rather publicity. A fair deal the way I describe it above.

Do you have specific knowledge or expertise that you could share with others? If so, you can establish yourself as an author and publish articles on the Internet. Publishing articles also creates credibility among peers and customers. Publishing articles is not only a very effective marketing tool, it is also cost effective. Think over what you know and start sharing it. The return on investment will come in the form of increased Web traffic and an enhanced reputation.

Eleven Quick Tips to Up Return Traffic to Your Site

Sometimes you need a kick start to get you off the ground when promoting your new business Web site. Use these 11 tips to get started. A combination of several tips will most likely guarantee return visitors to your Web site. Return visitors most likely mean more sales.

1. **Build a solid business foundation:**
   Before starting. Create a business plan (you should revisit this document every quarter), marketing plan, client profile, and a site map for your Web site.

2. **Be very consistent**:
   Brand your company and stick to it.

3. **Create acceptable and easy to understand policies:**
   Build trust by implementing Customer Service, a Code of Ethics, and a Privacy Policy.

4. **Network locally:**
   Bring local people to your site by getting in contact with the people nearest you – your neighbors. Start with the local Chamber of Commerce, for example.

5. **Place the URL address everywhere:**
   Put the address to your Web site on all your printed business literature: business cards, brochures, newsletters, letterhead, invoices, ads, etc.!

6. **Offer added value:**
   related to your business and the ideal client (target group). A solid resource database helping clients get the most out of your services could be a good start. Offer products such as FTP software for a Web hosting client. This makes perfect sense because your

clients can use it to conveniently upload their files to the hosting Web server.

7. **Use a "Recommend This Site to a Friend" script:**
   Put it on your site. If someone visits your site and knows someone else who may appreciate it, this feature will e-mail the pages link to the recipient. Easy access to a tool like this could increase 'word of mouth' advertising.

8. **Set up monthly chats:**
   Start threads about various topics or install bulletin boards (forums) to build relationships and community. This will attract customers to your business. Invite industry-specific experts to a chat so that they can answer customer questions. This is a perk nobody can resist.

9. **Share your knowledge with others:**
   Teach classes in colleges or schools or speak to groups about subjects relating to your products and services. Students suddenly turn into customers and/or spread the word ....

10. **Conduct periodic contests:**
    Announce the winners on your site. As a Web host, you could have contest for the best Web design on your servers. People like to show off. Use this behavior to attract new clients.

11. **Participate in online forums as an expert:**
    But do not SPAM the forums with your advertising messages. Use your signature to quietly promote your services. Once people see you as a valuable member with lots of information and start trusting you, they will start trusting you with their business.

Making Your Web Site More Successful

Building a Web site and getting it online is easy. Attracting visitors to it is the more difficult part. Most people are not patient enough when it comes to building up traffic. They expect thousands of visitors a week right after they go live with their Web site. But that is not how it works. I want to share some secrets of how to make your Web site more successful.

Provide Content

Search engines love content. The more content you can provide, the better off you are. Don't put all the content on one page. Spread the content across many pages. The reason for this is that every page gets spidered separately by Google and other search engines. Each page of yours in their index is an additional chance that your link gets listed in somebody's search results. Quality content is more valuable to search engines since they want to provide real information to visitors. Search engines do not want to refer to link farms or redirects. If they can refer a customer directly to the most valuable content, all the better for the search engine. Search engines live off of providing good results.

Domain Name

Do not use a domain name like:

www.freewebpages.com/~yourname

Search engines don't like these kinds of links. Plus these links don't look very professional. It makes it look like you are cheap and either are not willing to pay for a more professional site or, even worse, you can't afford one. It also prevents you from building a brand name (your ultimate goal).

Spend the $9.00 per year for your own domain name. It's money well spent.

KISS

Keep it simple, silly! The simpler the better. Here is a rule of thumb: text content should outweigh the html content. The pages should be W3 validated and work in Internet Explorer as well as Mozilla's Firefox. If you get too fancy, some search engine spiders might not be able to read your pages. Look at Google, eBay or Yahoo. They all have a simple design, are easy to navigate, and people are flocking to them. If you use sub-directories, the directory names should be descriptive (for example, "steel-products" or "paper-clips"). The same is true for your pages. If you are able to give each page a descriptive name, you will better off in the long run. Web site performance is critical. If your pages load too slowly, your business will suffer. Make sure the Web site sits on a fast Web server and that the page sizes are 20K or less. If you can keep page sizes to 15K or less you are ahead of the curve.

Pace Yourself

Build one content page per day or at least three to four per week. You may think you do not have that many products. But establish yourself as a source of products or industry related information. If customers can learn from the content you provide, they will respect you and your business and this will lead them to use your services and products, too. Pages with 300-600 words should be more than sufficient.

Keywords

Make sure you use important keywords in the title of each topic and through out the text without looking like a SPAMMER (meaning, do not go overboard with keywords). Find out what the important keywords for your business are.

Outbound Links

Search engines love to see outbound links every once in a while. It proves to a search engine that your Web site is related to a certain topic and industry. Make sure you use a keyword for the link and not just the plain URL. Linking to http://www.webhostingresourcekit.com is less valuable than linking to the same site as Web Hosting Help. The keywords here are "Web Hosting Help".

In-site Cross Links

I'm not done with linking to other places yet. In-site cross links (links from one page of your Web site to another page on your Web site) will be an important part of the future of your Web site. Imagine article "A" getting a lot of feedback and many external sites linking to it. This article page will receive a higher page rank than other pages on your Web site. This cross link will now share the page rank out to the other pages of your Web site and will, therefore eventually, boost the page rank of the page linked to.

Submit to Search Engines

You've built your Web site and are ready to go live. How will search engines find your new Web site? Unless you link to the new Web site from an existing Web site, you will have to let search engines know about it. Submit the Web site to: Google, Altavista, WiseNut, DirectHit, and Hotbot (and every other one you know). Also submit the Web site to DMOZ. I'd personally stay away from paid listings unless you think it is necessary. Anyway, now comes the tough part, forget about the submissions. It might take a few weeks or months for a site to be spidered.

Web Server Logging / Web Site Tracking

To be able to use your Web site properly, you will need good logging tools. You want to know how many Web site visitors you get, where they come from, what pages they look at, and how long they stay. A counter on your Web site does not do it. You need tools like Webalizer, AWStats, Urchin or Webtrends. If your Web host does not provide any of the first three options (Webtrends is fee-based) you should move to a new Web host. Proper log file analysis is important to your success.

High Search Engine Rankings - A Long Term Strategy

The last 1.5 years have shown major changes in search engine behavior across the board. Algorithms change at random dates. Websites that ranked great in search results are suddenly completely wiped out from the search index. It becomes less and less predictable what a certain change to your website will get for results. A major change to a website or the way how it is promoted could have a major impact on search engine success for that website.

Webmasters need to gear to up to stay ahead of the game. As changes cannot easily be reversed to re-establish search engine ranking a website could be dead in the water for 3-6 months before it eventually recovers. It might actually not recover at all and becomes dead internet real estate. The difficulty every webmaster is facing - each major search engine uses different criteria to judge a website and how high it will be listed in search results. Success in MSN does not necessarily mean success in Google or Yahoo and vice versa.

To further see the impact of search engine changes one also has to consider who is affected most. The "aggressive" webmaster with lots of affiliate shopping websites and websites mainly build to generate advertising income will certainly see a different impact compared to a webmaster that is going a much more conservative way. There is a major difference in building a website for short-term success (or mid-term for the matter in Internet terms) and in building a website for long-term success.

Search engines will (or partially already have) develop filters to sort out websites with certain type of content or that promote certain type of services. This way they hope to increase the quality of the search results and to provide better quality of service to their clients/visitors.

Webmasters looking for long-term success need to change the way in which they operate to succeed. Unless you have a lot of money you can throw at the problem (advertising, marketing), you need to work very conservative in regards to search engine optimization and how to achieve high search engine listings/rankings. Plan projects a long time in advance. Buy domain names way ahead of schedule and place some content on them to get them indexed and accounted for. A domain name being 2 years old or more (and indexed for that period) is more valuable than a 2 week old domain name registration with some duplicate content.

Slowly build back links to the new domain. Search engines seem to be looking at back links in a way that a large increase of back links in a very short period is less valuable or reason to suspect brute force search engine optimization (brute force SEO) which can result in complete removal from the search index. So, a strategy of slowly increasing the number of back links is more desirable and will be more effective for the long-term success. Do not do anything on a website that does not look 'natural' in regards to growth.

Adding 1,000+ pages in a day does not look natural. Adding 25 pages of content over a week looks much more natural. Time does a good thing. A site becomes more popular and receives more back links. With the increased popularity an increase in the growth rate does not look as much problematic anymore. Now adding 50 pages of content in a week just matches the overall growth rate much better. And again - time passes by and the popularity goes up (ideal case). An increase in adding back links and content just looks more natural.

This sort of natural or organic growth will be important to achieve search engine success in the future. The second key is good, high quality content and easy to read URLs for each page.

A combination of these two key ingredients will almost guarantee success in how your website is going to be ranked in search engines.

The Story of My Own Business

I sn 2002, I founded Net Services USA LLC and became a Web host. This is the story of how I started my business and which turns it took.

Early 2002, I was sick of being a corporate slave and wanted to work for myself. However, I did not have enough money to buy an existing business or to invest heavily into a brand-new business. I worked as a computer system administrator for a large corporation and was tired of doing that work for someone else.

I had computer skills and access to the Internet all day long. "So, why not do something computer-related when starting a business?!" I said to myself. I already owned a couple of domain names which I was hosting in a multi-domain Web hosting account. It was what is known as a reseller account. The actual Web host provided full-time tech support and I could host as many domains as I wanted on this account as long as they fit into the allotted bandwidth and disk space.

Many Web designers and new Web hosts were already using these kinds of hosting accounts to start their own business. It was cost-effective and offered one the opportunity to concentrate on sales, marketing, and customer service and to leave the technical part to the Web host administrator in the background. All I needed was one of these reseller accounts (in fact, I already had one) and I could start my own Web hosting business right at that very moment.

I registered my business with the State of Colorado. My research had shown that a LLC would be the best business model for me and my current situation. It would protect my personal assets and make it look like a legit business, in other words, professional. It took me a week to figure out a good name for my business, though. One requirement was that the domain should also still be available. As I also love my country, I wanted to express this by having the word "USA" integrated into the business name. Net Services USA LLC was the result. On the same day, I registered my business with the State of Colorado; I opened a bank account and made a deposit for $1,000, the money I needed to get started. I also got a P.O. Box at the local post office. I was ready to do business (well, not really but read on ...).

What next? I registered the domain name for my business and made a list of things I would need to run the business. I needed to build a Web site and I needed some sort of a merchant account for credit card processing. I also wanted to resell domain names. My research took me to OpenSRS / Tucows as the first choice for domain reselling. Their pricing was not the least expensive but they offered excellent tools for the reseller and the actual clients. They had a small application fee that I needed to pay, but that was not a big deal. I signed up with them and my application was approved in no time.

Now I had to decide how I wanted to charge credit cards. A real credit card merchant account was too expensive and would have required me to enter a minimum 12-month contract. In my case that would have drained my resources much too quickly. A monthly fee of around $35.00 just did not seem to be appropriate yet. I decided to use a third party service offered by 2Checkout (www.2checkout.com). They would do the actual credit card processing through their Web site for fees a little bit above the processing fees of a regular merchant account. But this was acceptable to me. I had no contract requirements and no monthly payments with them. Everything was covered through the processing fees. They would also do some basic fraud checking, too.

I started building my Web site and as I am not such a good programmer, I had a friend help me implement the credit card processing part. Two weeks later, I was ready to open the Web site for business. It felt good to have accomplished so much in such a short time.

Now all I needed were paying customers. I had already submitted my page to several search engines and now started submitting it to Web hosting directories. I searched for business directories online and listed my homepage wherever it was free to submit my site. Traffic on the Web site slowly increased but I did not get any signups. That was a little disconcerting. "But - I have to be patient." became my mantra.

I visited other Web hosting companies on the Internet and compared their pricing and features to mine. My pricing was good and competitive, but probably still too high. I reduced my prices a little bit and finally got the first signup. $4.00 a month for a 1 GB bandwidth Web hosting account. It was awesome. Even if it was only one small account, the whole thing motivated me incredibly. I knew I was on the right path.

Shortly after receiving the signup message from my Web site, I had the account created. I wrote a welcome message and send it to the customer. Everything looked good now. I had my first customer and I was sure many more would follow.

The Web host I was leasing my reseller account from grew bigger and bigger. But unfortunately support-wise the problems grew as well. The server my account was on seemed to be overloaded with accounts. Downtime and sluggish response was a sure sign of problems. The helpdesk denied any problems and always blamed it on me. I still hesitated to move somewhere else and hoped things would improve.

I got a couple more clients during the following weeks and things were slowly taking off. I had already made some money and my basic expenses were covered. I decided to pay for some advertising in a local computer newspaper and placed an ad in their classified section for four weeks. I has hoped for at least 4 or 5 new customers from of this, but the result was zero. I noticed slightly higher visitor numbers, but no sign-ups at all. It was very frustrating to see money go down the drain.

In the meantime, the server performance had gotten worse and I decided to move while it was still possible and before any clients left. I researched the market for a better reseller account. I still did not want to rent my own server as that would have required a greater investment and a commitment I was not ready for yet. I also would have to look into getting some technical help, as I am not really an experienced Linux administrator (I am mainly a Windows person). All those things would have eaten up my small profits and my savings. I just needed a little more time. I had seen too many Web hosts disappear and I had read too many horror stories on Web hosting-related forums. Every problem host got his/her 15 minutes of (bad) fame. I wanted to grow my business slowly based on a stable foundation.

After a few days, it looked like I had found a good new reseller Web host, a company based in the UK with servers in the USA. A busy support forum showed positive signs and positive feedback from the clients. I signed up and started moving my own sites over. On a Sunday afternoon (US time), my Web sites and the whole server disappeared from the Internet. No support calls were answered. A visit to the customer forum showed many frustrated customers all with the same problem. What had happened? The support person for the shift on Sunday had fallen asleep. Nothing had woken him up. This was unacceptable and so I decided to move again. I had only my own sites to move at this point. I decided to go with the second choice of my research and what a difference that made. The support was top notch. It was always available and every support request was answered in less than two hours.

I was happy with my choice and so were my customers. I had properly explained the problems I was experiencing and offered a valid solution for everyone. I also threw in a month of free Web hosting or upgraded the account to the next higher package to make the clients happy. Within two weeks everything was moved over and I could close the account with the unreliable Web host.

Things ran smoothly from then on. As I did not do much marketing, the number of sign-ups was very low but that was all right with me. It gave me time to concentrate on the existing customers and to build up a good and solid reputation. I still had my full-time job, too.

I frequently checked my Web sites and made changes to pricing and modified the design until I was totally satisfied with it. I knew I could not compete with all the $1.00 hosts out there or with companies offering 10 GB of bandwidth for less than $10.00 a month. So, I put the emphasis on my services and the quality of my products my customers could expect.

I tried some paid advertising again but the results were not good. I realized that my higher prices did not meet the requirements of the audience I had targeted. So I changed my strategies a little bit. I concentrated on small businesses in my local community. I designed a flyer with a special and every time I saw a business truck or business car parked at my local Home Depot or grocery store, I took a flyer and put it under the windshield wiper of that car or truck. The results were good. I reached a 40% return rate and a 15% conversion rate using this kind of advertising.

I reached a point where I could justify the expense of having my own credit card merchant account. This would reduce processing fees in the long run and would be more convenient for me. I could collect the credit card numbers and charge my clients manually or via scripts. No more redirecting to 2Checkout.com needed. It would also show my business name on the credit card statements of my clients. This would look much more professional.

After doing some research, I signed up with a company from the East Coast (USA). I paid a $189.00 application fee and got access to Authorize.Net, a very large credit card processing gateway on the Internet. My monthly costs (fixed) were supposed to be $25.95, which included $1,000 of processing volume a month before additional processing fees would be added on top of that. I had asked numerous questions about this upfront, but when the first bill arrived, I saw a monthly fee of $35.95 as my monthly minimum. My questions for the vendor remained unanswered. As I was locked into a 1-year contract, I didn't have much choice. I had additional money invested in software scripts and labor to get everything integrated and any delay would have cost me more than that $10 extra a month.

Now that I had everything in place, I waited for more business to roll in. But the economy still seemed to be in the toilet. Large corporations were making money but Joe Consumer was still hesitating to pay for quality Web hosting services. New business sign-ups were random. I did pick up some Web design clients and even a few IT consulting clients. This helped increase my income level quite a bit. One Web hosting customer left and moved to his own server.

I had reached the income level of a good part-time business. Two hours of work a day and I was making some decent money via Web hosting and Web design.

80% of my clients were from the USA. 50% of my clients were from my local town. I wanted to expand and one good way would be to not only offer services in a different language but also offer support the same way. Being a fluent speaker of German, I decided to offer a Web site in German for the folks in Germany, Switzerland, and Austria. A friend of mine living in Germany at that time agreed to help with support during the (my) night and so I had a good foundation to start a second business Web site. I could provide 24/7 support to my clients this way.

The new Web site was build, and since I was a member of several German-speaking online communities, I used the opportunity to advertise my services through my signature. This worked pretty well and I received a couple of sign-ups.

The situation with my full-time job took a turn for the worst. Local management actually motivated us to look for new jobs. But my own business was not yet ready to take the big jump. In the summer of 2003, I found a new job. The salary was at the same high level as my current salary, so I decided to accept the job offer. Soon I realized that I no longer had the freedom to support my customers during the day. Internet access at the new office was limited and monitored. As mentioned before, my own business was still too small for full self-employment and being used to a high salary from the corporate job, it did not make it easier.

That was the point where I had to make a decision, so I decided to sell my hosting clients and concentrate on my full-time job and perhaps do some Web design here and there. I could have hired somebody but that would have taken away all the revenue I had generated and I was not sure if I could find someone trustworthy enough to continue the service I had provided. World-class customer service was important to me. It also would not have taken off any stress or pressure (time-wise). Also the overhead with accounting, payroll, and all that stuff. I don't know if I really wanted to do it. I just did not feel connected enough to this kind of business. Being available 24/7 and all that stuff. I don't think I was ready for that. I do not mind working hard and going the extra mile but this kind of business would have required a commitment I was not yet ready to make . I guess I was also making too much money at my regular job at that time to be hungry enough to take jump and become self-employed.

I put the business on the market and I received plenty of offers. I was surprised and had to back-off a little bit, as I had not had enough time to prepare my books and balance sheet for a potential buyer. After reviewing all the offers I had received, not a single one was worth a cent. This was frustrating especially after having made the decision to sell the business. I had made my money and offered the business basically for free if the person who would take over met my strict conditions. I found a couple of qualified business owners who wanted to add additional customers to their client base and they offered a fair amount of money in return for the clients. A few weeks later all the terms were worked out and I turned over my clients, including the server space to make the move easier. I signed up for a new reseller account and moved my own domains over. It was over. the stress was gone and I felt relieved.

It took only a few days until the first client came back and asked for help. The new host had a different philosophy in regards to customer service. Apparently he had not told me the truth. It took only another week or two and the next client complained. He even asked if I would take him back or knew another host and Web designer for him. I felt bad for these people. All my research I had done was basically down the drain. I e-mailed the new host and things improved for a while. The bad service and very slow response time of the new host soon returned.

The client, who had asked before, asked again if I would be able to help and I took him back as a client with the idea that it would help me pay for my own hosting and anyway, one client was not a big deal. I also had a couple of friends who paid me a little money for hosting their Web sites, so it just fit together.

Things ran along smoothly for two more months. Then more complaints about the new host came in. Up to that point, he had not billed anyone. Nothing. My e-mail messages remained unanswered. As he was using my domain name to provide the DNS service, I finally e-mailed and told him that I would take my domain name back. That caused him finally to reply. His reply was:

"I have realized I made a mistake in taking over your customers. I have spent many dollars in phone calls to try to satisfy some of the customers. Some are not happy that the accounts were transferred to another company. I really don't want the customers anymore. I have been trying to figure out how to get rid of them. ......Do you know anyone who would like the customers? Would you like them back? I need to turn them over to someone else. What would you suggest? ......Let me know if you have any suggestions. The only thing I can think of if you don't want them back is tell them a date when I will stop hosting their account and they would have to set up at another company. I wish there was a better way. Let me know if you have any ideas. "

Unbelievable. I e-mailed him and explained my point of view and that he should at least shut down with dignity. It was not the customers' fault. My e-mail must have triggered something and he changed his mind. Time went by and 6 weeks later the whole thing started again. I was sick of it. I took control over my domain name and gave him DNS entries for his clients. I then informed the buyer about it. He had never stuck to the agreement and no payments had ever arrived after the initial turnover.

Then he complained to me that I could have broken the lines of communication between him and the clients. This was very unprofessional. I showed him his old e-mail messages, including all the details. Clients had also told me that he had never billed them properly and that a check sent to him had never been cashed.

So, was that it?

In the spring of 2004, I realized that I was not happy with how things were going. Sure, I made good money from my job as a computer system administrator but it was not satisfying at all. I stepped back from everything I was doing and re-evaluated my situation. I came to the conclusion that building and operating my own business was still what I wanted to do.

I looked at my business plan again and at the things that were bothering me in the past. Sure, Web hosting is a great thing to do but the 24/7 availability requirement of the job AND the business had taken a toll on me. I did not really wanted to be available 24/7 again. I had to change my business strategy to make this happen. I still had a few Web hosting customers and so

I decided to continue doing Web hosting but on a much smaller scale than before.

My new plan included Web hosting to cover my basic costs of doing business and maybe a little more. A very hand-selected group of clients with small requirements for support would be the basis of my "new" business. Since I had a great deal of business knowledge, I decided to use this in a different way, by providing information to a targeted group of people would be a first step for my business at this point. The "Webhostingreport.net" was born. I build the Web site to provide business information and tutorials for Web hosts. The Web site would generate income from advertising and a subscription-based membership. The model worked quite well for a while but outgrew its platform fairly quick. The learning curve for this new business model was steep and I made mistakes. But this time, I was more aggressive in working around those mistakes and fixing them. Especially the last three months of 2004 became an experience I would not have wanted to miss. I learned so many business related things at such a high pace that I was able to generate most of my business income during those last three months of the year.

In November of 2004, I decided to change my strategy a little bit, so I added a new Web site to my network of Web sites. The "Web Hosting Resource Kit" would be the new platform for all my hosting related efforts. The domain name "Webhostingresourcekit.com" was better suited for marketing and much more descriptive. I decided to spend the money necessary to get the new platform ready for the expected growth and to be prepared this time around. Being more pro-active should help me avoid many of the costly mistakes I had experienced in the experimental part of the last 6 months. I purchased some expensive article management software and built the Web site around it. The Web site went live in early December of 2004 and just four weeks later I was able to pay off my investment, so that from that point on, the Web site was generating real profits.

So I basically missed out on the chance of doing proper business for the first half of 2004, but then I shifted into very high gear and turned things around. I am very proud that in 2004, my business still produced a profit (after tax) in the $x,xxx.xx range. I learned more about running my own business in six months than I did in the entire time before. It sometimes takes a while to realize what we really like to do. Web Hosting is a great business, it just does not satisfy me totally and I think that was one of the problems I was facing. I think that was one of the reasons why I was not 100% committed. I now have a much better understanding of what I want and where I want to go. Net Services USA LLC is well positioned now and the first half of 2005 is very promising. Business is great. It just took a while to find out for myself ….

And here is a little piece of advice from one who started out being a Web host. You will never know how things are until you try them. There is no shame in realizing that a certain job or certain business is not what you want to do. It's what you do with that knowledge and how you steer through the curve balls life throws at you.

Web Hosting-
Related Addresses

Here is a short but sweet list of interesting Web sites that will give you even more information about getting into the Web hosting business:

http://www.Webhostingresourcekit.com

http://www.Webhostingreport.net

http://www.smallbusinessland.com

http://www.tucows.com

http://www.enom.com

http://www.webhostingtalk.com

http://www.sitepoint.com

http://www.hosthideout.com

http://www.2checkout.com

http://www.authorize.net

http://www.ev1servers.net

http://www.1and1.com

http://www.httpme.com

http://www.voxtreme.com

http://www.httptalk.com

http://www.small-business-forum.com

http://www.sba.gov

http://www.vistaprint.com

http://www.gotprint.com

http://www.usps.com

http://www.nolo.com

Index